SPIRITUAL LYRICS

By Antonio Finn

DISCLAIMER:

**This book contains typos and other grammatical errors.
I pondered correcting them, but opted to leave them as they are
to maintain authenticity to who I was when I wrote them.**

I hope you read beyond the text and feel my intent.

-   Antonio

Copyright © 2023 by Antonio Finn
All rights reserved. No portion of this book may be reproduced in any form without permission from the author, except as permitted by U.S. copyright law.
For permissions contact the author.

First Edition: 2023
Printed in the United States of America
ISBN: 9-798218-050092

DEDICATION

In loving memory of my loving Mother and Grandmother, Rosie Jean Williams and Bennie May Williams.

THE COMPLETE PICTURE PROCESS

Spiritual Lyrics

One day a brother told me

a scenario of a picture.

We can't tell what it is going to be.

It may be a figure.

People always assume

you will not make it,

but I know you can.

It's our little secret.

You hypocrites sit around daily

looking for a void in Christians

like watching a Polaroid.

Now something is being revealed.

Are you still seeking fault?

I'm open to God,

just like someone who opened a bank vault.

The Polaroid before your eyes

is becoming clearer.

I'm keeping things in prayer to God.

I want to be nearer.

You may laugh.

Antonio Finn

Now God will laugh at you

Much later the devil is using you well,

but my God is still greater.

I may not look like much,

or you don't like the way I act daily.

It's becoming much clearer,

and that's a fact.

I'm glad I don't put my trust in man,

but in my maker.

So why judge people?

Who do I look like to you?

A creator God will take care of us.

We're so special and obsolete.

The Polaroid has been revealed.

It's me, so rejoice

and ignore what people say about you.

God sees the finished product

as if it's already complete.

Amen.

God Almighty is not prejudiced.

Spiritual Lyrics

In the world today,

People hate the color of one's skin.

This is a very touchy subject for many,

so where do we begin?

How about starting with yourself?

Is one drop in you?

Can you help someone

if they're of a different race?

If not, "tsk, tsk."

Let me tell you something that is real.

Heaven can't have hate.

You walk around with a cape

and a hat hiding your face,

but you can't hide from God.

You fools didn't know that, I guess.

You get initiated by

shaving your heads and making gestures.

I pray God will make these acts

be sour possibly like a lemon.

You blindly express the words

Antonio Finn

of Latinos, Blacks, or White power.

Sorry, fellas, you all are very deceived.

There's only one power,

and none of you have it.

I'm telling you

God Almighty isn't prejudiced.

You say it isn't in the Scriptures. Oh yes, it is.

Just look in the Scriptures.

Oh, I forgot that you quit a long time ago.

I'll give you book, chapter, and verse.

It's John 4:20.

Instead of hating, name-calling, and killing,

grab the Word and eat it up.

There's plenty.

If you don't, and you're still prejudiced,

you're going where it's never windy –

just balls of fire and the sparkle of flames.

Your eyes are finally open in the abyss.

Imagine when you were a kid.

You didn't see color and weren't prejudiced.

Spiritual Lyrics

You joyfully played hide-n-seek

with Chinese, Blacks, and Spanish kids.

You're desperate now

and plead with the Lord

that you can do better, but wait.

I'll learn to get along with my fellow man.

I've changed.

I'll walk a clean slate.

I'll go to church and pay my tithes.

"Quiet, my son. I love you, but it's too late.

You're hell bound now,

and so are many others

who hate gays and profess

that they love Me, but they hate.

Those aren't My ways.

I don't teach or delight in hate.

Young and old men and women

won't live out half their days.

For it is written,

'How can you say you love Me,

Antonio Finn

who you haven't seen,

but hate your brother who you have seen?'"

Thus says the Lord.

Just look around at the blue skies

that don't mind the white clouds

hanging out with them

and the many colors of the rainbow.

These colors don't mind blending together.

How about the black clouds

that drop clear rain on the green grass?

Look at the many colors of nature

and the many different races He created.

If you're still blind,

find a star, a planet, or the moon.

He died for us all regardless of our color,

so if you bleed red blood and do God's will,

you're my sister and my brother.

God Almighty is not prejudiced.

Amen.

Devil, you're a liar.

Spiritual Lyrics

I bind ya, devil,

And another thing,

You make me sick.

My brothers and my sister

When you're just about to quit,

And you've done all that you can do,

Get down on your knees

And ask God for the strength

To put up with it.

Remember God will answer

Not when you want him to.

I promise you this: "Gotta get it."

What can I possibly do

when the bills come in like a flood

and are due?

It seems like you never can get caught up.

It's difficult to find anyone

to give you any assistance.

Can you trust their word or reliability?

Man, I'm tired of going through it.

Antonio Finn

Sorry, I'm just having a fit.

I must remember I can't, I gotta get it.

There's not any food in the fridge.

It's looking kind of slim.

I got a letter saying support is

past due for my son.

In reality, I can't support him.

Whatever happened to my cup runneth over?

It's not even close to the rim.

In a couple of days, the car note is goin' to be due.

I wouldn't dare ask anybody for nothing,

because folks act so brand new.

This is why I'm asking you

for something that could tide me over

Maybe a grand or two.

Please, can you make it quick?

Foolish thoughts in mind say,

"Man, go sell one brick, you know."

Spiritual Lyrics

CAUTION, UNDERGOING CONSTRUCTION

Antonio Finn

Today the Lord woke me up.

I'll thank him.

The sign in my mind reads,

"Up ahead caution, undergoing construction."

That's letting me know

He's going to be moving some things

out of my life that may cause self-destruction.

I heard a voice say, "Son, follow My instruction.

You're going to have various trials,

but I'm going to bring you out of every one.

They'll help you to have strength

in your weak areas.

I love you so.

I'll be there through them all,

because I'm God, and I've already won.

My child, this may hurt a little bit,

but your anger has got to go.

I think I'll use this bulldozer.

Oh, quit crying like a baby.

You're a man now.

Spiritual Lyrics

Why won't you act like it?

You've gotten older.

Get whatever off your chest right now,

and give it to Me.

Let's not forget that chip on your shoulder.

Give Me those lustful, wicked, murderous thoughts.

I'll tell you what I'm gonna do.

I'll mix them in this concrete after it dries.

I'll cast them into the sea of forgetfulness.

I won't bring it back up.

Neither should you.

Hey, this is fun.

I don't need any man,

because I'm the one-man construction crew.

Watch out for My awesome wrecking ball.

Smash that thing around.

Your heart has taken a great fall.

Finally, My love can penetrate your heart

just like a jackhammer does concrete.

Now I'll become your all-in-all.

Antonio Finn

I'll take your pride, shame, and fear.

Take my steamroller, so they'll be pressed down.

Lord, I'll let go of the wheel, so you can steer.

Let go and let God.

I believe every time I do that,

all the saints, You, and Jesus begin to cheer.

Lord, let's not forget all my worries,

anxiety, and stress.

Lord, I know You give,

but today do most of the taking.

You knew I needed it all done.

Rip, tear, smash, and break

in order for me to do Your will

and be just like You.

I'm glad I don't do it, but You do all of my making.

Spiritual Lyrics

DOUBLE UP

Antonio Finn

I'm sitting here, and I'm still awake.

That's 'cause I'm keeping my promise.

I can't take a break.

I got mad work to do.

It wouldn't get it done

if I left it up to you.

Cluadell don't need a crew,

'cause I'm grown up now,

and I got my own shoes.

Guess I better double up

even though they played for keeps.

'Twas a big change to a cold, hard bunk.

I wasn't sleepy.

Take my advice.

Call your peeps if you're needy,

'cause cons and crooks love to take from you.

They're greedy.

I think it was in the fall

that I got into a conflict with some tall dude.

He was sizin' me up.

Spiritual Lyrics

We had a fallout on the step.

I quit and walked away from him,

but he still wanted to fight.

I said, "No."

He quit.

I'm in this stank ol' cell.

I ain't feelin' well.

Oh, Lord, I can't take this no mo'.

I can't just jump over this rail.

I've changed my mind now,

'cause it's not worth it.

Here comes the mail.

It's from my kid.

He's asking when I'm coming home.

That's hard.

He wants to know when I'm getting out of jail

and what I did.

Should I tell him?

Man, they grow up so fast and get so big.

How foolish and stupid I was back then.

Antonio Finn

I was selling drugs and shacking up

in my little shack.

I snorted my smack, thinking to get rid

of the pain in my neck and back.

I messed up and was found guilty.

I wish I could throw it in the rear.

I can't concentrate on that

'cause where I'm goin'

I can't have no fear.

I gotta survive

'cause I don't know if death is near.

I made it 'cause of Almighty God.

I'm still here.

I missed out on five,

but at least I'm still alive.

Hurry up, mash the gas till we arrive.

See, son, I told you I'll be home soon.

We had tears in our eyes.

then my son replied, "I love you, Daddy."

Son, I love you, too.

Spiritual Lyrics

His cheeks bubbled up.

I guess I better double up.

Antonio Finn

BLOOD RAW AND UNCUT (04-02)

Spiritual Lyrics

There's a time and place for everything

and a season.

I'm using this time to improve myself.

What's your reason?

Some people play games acting all tough,

but underneath they're flawed.

They say it ain't nothing but time.

Hold up.

It's time to give 'em something blood raw.

Jesus gave us the word,

so we don't have to go around in a rut.

Are you a fool or what?

I'm gonna give it to you blood raw and uncut.

After all the mockery and shame He suffered,

people are still having sex, doing drugs, lying,

drinking, and hanging with your boys or crew

actin' all crazy like they're death struck

killin' up folk.

Satan got something up his sleeve.

The things we do and say.

Antonio Finn

Oh, what tangled webs we often weave.

Our Master and Savior bled, cried tears

and had unspeakable pain after they mocked Him and

plucked out His beard.

He died then finally we got our gain.

I don't know about you,

but when I snorted powder,

it gotta be uncut.

I almost lost my life fooling around with that junk.

No if's, ands, or buts.

Spiritual Lyrics

GIVE ME THAT GOOD OL' STUFF.

Antonio Finn

It makes me feel tingly all over.

It cleans anything up better than Clorox bleach

cutting both ways down to the marrow,

so what's good for you also is good for me.

Oh, Lord, help us to live right

and open up to you more.

On the other hand, it's free.

It was bought with the price of blood

which we can never pay back,

so it's priceless.

Your marriage gone bad and can't get a job?

No problems are too big for God.

Give me that good stuff.

The King James Bible is purest of them all.

It's purer than a Cuban's half or quarter key.

I won't have to rob anyone to get it.

All I gotta to do is read my Bible.

Yum yum, give me some.

Just two more chapter, and I'm full blood

brought and bought the way for all of us

Spiritual Lyrics

Raw is how they did Jesus

because when we sin,

it's just like crucifying him all over again.

Please don't cuss.

There's still hope if you slip.

Repent and get right back in the saddle

'cause this war can last awhile.

It's spiritual.

Just keep this in mind.

Thank Him for the cleansing words.

Read them, and don't forget to pray.

I fought my good fight.

Get my white robe

and walk down the gold path.

Don't get that watered-down stuff

that people have already touched.

Instead get the blood raw and uncut.

Amen.

Antonio Finn

HE'S COMIN' BACK

Spiritual Lyrics

One day my Lord ascended into the clouds,

but don't you worry,

because He's comin' back soon.

I can hear some of ya sayin',

"Yeah, yeah, yeah.

I've heard that before for years.

If He's comin', then where is He?"

Why do you let the devil attack your mind like that?

Believe me, now isn't the time to slack.

Don't let Him catch ya

with your work undone

and worryin' about your family

and friends talkin' about you.

Come on with me to church.

I know that all our friends

and family members won't be saved.

There's nothin' wrong with carin' about 'em,

but make sure you're where you belong.

No one knows when God's Son is comin' back.

That's why you better work out your own salvation.

Antonio Finn

Is this helpin' you any?

Please make the right choice to serve Him,

'cause this decision will affect you for the duration.

It's according to where you want

to spend the rest of your life,

so it's not a joking matter.

Just see the chapter on Revelations.

Hey, that's up to you if you really

want to be left behind here on Earth.

If I were you, I'd start prayin' fast

and get your house in order,

'cause we have so much trouble

obeyin' the Lord.

Time is getting' shorter, and this isn't the time

for nobody to be playing around.

I can hear some of ya sayin',

"Yeah, yeah, yeah. I've heard that before for years,

and if He is then where is He?"

If you're not prepared for His return,

it's time that you packed.

Spiritual Lyrics

You want Him to see that your work is done

and not catch you takin' a nap.

If you don't know by now,

I'll tell ya again.

He's comin' back.

Antonio Finn

12-19-04 HIDDEN TALENTS

Spiritual Lyrics

Hey, everybody has at least one,

and it's deep down inside.

You just gotta do some diggin'.

For heaven sakes, don't give up looking,

For God has blessed everybody on earth

with at least one talent.

If you don't want yours, give it to me.

I'll cast lots for it, or I'll start the auction biddin'.

Have you heard about the talent story in the Bible?

It says that whatever God blesses you with

unto Him you must give all the praise and glory.

If you don't, something bad might happen to you.

Something may go horribly wrong.

In the story, a servant hid and buried it.

His master went away

on a very long journey.

The wise servants remembered

What their master said.

They carried it out.

The one who collected money

Antonio Finn

strived to increase it,

and so he's doubled it.

Another sold his cattle and bulls at a sizable profit.

As you probably already know

the one who had two talents

turned them into four.

Another servant, who had five,

turned his into ten.

If you do nothing with your talent,

that's a sin.

If for some odd reason you didn't catch on

to what I was sayin',

where have you been?

Do you remember the foolish servant

who hid his talent?

When his master returned,

he saw that his servant had been disobedient,

so he gave his talent

to one of the other men.

Let me ask you a personal question.

Spiritual Lyrics

On a scale of one to ten, where do you stand?

Please remember that God

gets all the glory and praise daily.

What will you do with your talent?

Hopefully, you won't bury your treasure.

I'm just speakin' the truth,

and if I've offended you in any way, I apologize.

If you don't like my bold gestures,

I'm sorry again.

If you've read this up until this point,

you're under the spotlight

and under a lot of pressure.

That's right.

You can't say that you haven't been warned

about your bad habits.

Make them disappear.

Please do something positive

with your hidden talents.

Antonio Finn

THE GATE

Spiritual Lyrics

The reason I talk like this

is because God is hardly talked about.

He's the real reason why you're seeing another one.

It's not a big ol' party.

You have got it all confused with a Mardi Gras,

and I'm quite sorry

that you had a hard pill to swallow.

My God, we made it,

and it's all because of You.

I can't believe that it's another

year we made it through,

'cause last year was so hard for us all.

Now the Lord is bringing in the new year,

and loud screams are all I can hear.

Some people really believe it's just fun and games,

so they just pop beers,

but some saints somewhere are shedding tears.

They wanted to give up,

so God stepped in and kept them on the right road.

God bless ya',

Antonio Finn

'cause you didn't veer off of the road.

Now that's somethin' to cheer about.

Happy new year.

Spiritual Lyrics

LOOKING DOWN AT THE GRASS

Antonio Finn

Lord, I am thankful that I am

looking down at the grass.

Somebody might not understand

what I mean in case they ask,

I'm glad that I'm still here.

I haven't gone on to the other side.

Someone last night wasn't so lucky.

Poor soul had dreams to accomplish.

They never had the chance

to change their goals.

Be thankful for living

'cause we don't know

when the good Lord will call

our number off of the scroll.

He can tell that heart to stop.

That blood which was warm

can become cold. That's why

I thank God for another day

after my life is made whole.

With my Father, I'll finally

Spiritual Lyrics

be able to rest in peace

forever with the Lord

instead of burning in hell.

Today, Lord, I'm looking down

at the grass and not looking up.

I can remember that time

when I didn't care about anything

when I was death struck.

I'm not supposed to be here today,

but You decided to spare me.

I know without You in my life,

I could've been cut short.

Look at the grass in the morning

when the sun bakes it.

In the evening, it's withered away.

That's why I'm not going to take

anything for granted.

Just like that grass,

we can be gone.

Do you get the big picture?

Antonio Finn

Think it over today.

Go figure out your calling.

Whenever He calls your name

to come home,

Somebody might not understand.

I'm glad that I'm still here

'cause just last night or

this morning some poor soul

passed on to the other side.

Lord, today I'm so glad that

I'm looking down at the grass.

Spiritual Lyrics

GOD'S NOT IN A BOTTLE (11-11-04)

Antonio Finn

I can't understand why people

think God is so small.

He's gone through hell,

but He still walked proud and tall.

Oh, no, my God's not in a bottle.

If He were, how could He tell His

disciples 'Wherever I lead, you follow.

I am the way. the truth, and the life.'

That's the Lord's motto.

If your Bible doesn't say that,

you may borrow mine.

If he was in a bottle,

how could He be by a newborn

or by the Roman guards

who tore His clothes?

How could He go see

dearly beloved friends

who died this morning?

How could He say to His people

that He's a strong tower?

Spiritual Lyrics

When things aren't quite

goin' your way.

It's okay, 'cause to Him

was given all power.

I can see my God 24/7

at any hour.

I know someone wants

me to put a lid on it.

No, I won't shut up.

I'm stubborn.

My head is really thick.

Sticks and stones may break….

Hey, what are you gonna do

with that stick?

It's almost time for me

to dodge that stick.

I used to run track.

I can run really quick.

Let's just say that

for some odd reason

Antonio Finn

I was a boat and

Along came bad weather,

and I ended up on a desert island.

How would I get help

from a bottle and a letter?

How would I know

the distance it needs to go?

I couldn't measure and

if God was small enough

to fit in a bottle,

what could He do to help

read my letter? Then

that would mean

we couldn't be together

forever and ever.

The Lord does a much better

reality check.

I know that your mind is a little bit boggled,

but now you get my point,

so awake now and goggle

Spiritual Lyrics

'cause my God's not in a bottle.

Antonio Finn

11-17-04 GOD HAS ALL POWER

Spiritual Lyrics

You don't have to worry

'cause God has all power.

He has to have it

to be our strong tower.

Especially when His people

call on Him for help

day and night, at any hour.

Do you know that He had

all power way back

at the time of His birth?

He used it to speak a word

to create the earth.

He created man from the dirt.

He gave us all the breath of life,

and ol' Adam became lonely,

so God created him a wife,

but He didn't intend for her

to cause any turmoil or strife

for her husband, Adam.

God has all power 'cause

Antonio Finn

with two fish and five loaves of bread,

He fed about five thousand.

He's even got the power to know

how many hairs that are on our heads.

They're numbered strand by strand.

He promised that a great man,

named Father Abraham,

would have so many children

he wouldn't be able

to count them all,

as many as the sea sand.

God has all power even

to make the dead rise again,

One Sabbath day

the Pharisees were in for

a really big surprise.

He has all power even

to heal the sick and

open blind eyes.

He has to have all power,

Spiritual Lyrics

Especially to hear

the broken-hearted cries.

He got power to take care

of any problem that you may have,

and size doesn't matter.

People, we must remember

to keep our eyes on the prize.

God has all power, if anything

gets in His way,

He's able to destroy and devour.

Things may not be goin'

so sweet for ya right

now or this hour.

That's fine.

Just get down on your knees,

and He'll make things sweet again.

If you need some shelter,

you need to run to the strong tower.

It doesn't matter what time

of the day or night.

Antonio Finn

He'll hear your cry at any hour.

My sisters and my brothers.

God has all power.

Spiritual Lyrics

MY LIFE INSIDE THE COCOON (APRIL 2, 2000)

Antonio Finn

I was living the life of destruction,

traveling in circles not knowing

which way I was going.

Hunting the sticky green alcohol,

lame to the brain, snorting cocaine

nothing but corruption.

I'm totting my place where

I'm from.

Ain't no peace.

Me against the world

'cause my dad is deceased.

I wished I could have known him more.

Often times I pray to ignore

all of my life struggles.

Ya know, pain, hurts.

Keep behind that door.

Now look where my

disobedience has gotten me.

It doesn't make any sense.

Hold up, my clothes are soaked.

Spiritual Lyrics

It's time for me to rinse.

Next time we need to listen

to an aunt, uncle, mother, or father.

If we had right now,

we'd be in the kitchen

stackin' it like you like it.

All da fixin's while ya'll

gettin' on with ya groove.

I'm eating rejected chicken,

Home-grown veggies, run-down

garbage, stale food.

For you who think you're bad,

just keep it up.

You'll end up in the cocoon.

Yeah, ain't goin' anywhere any time soon.

Uh huh, kind of like the caterpillar

all out doin' whatever,

then finally goes into metamorphosis.

He goes into that deep, dark lonely abyss.

"Tsk, tsk." Some say it's senseless,

Antonio Finn

but I don't.

When you're doing time by yourself

ya know alone.

Yeah, that's right.

I came in the cocoon,

so I can be still just like a stone.

I said it before, and I'll say it again.

This is my temporal home.

I'm goin' through the process of changing

and trying to use my time wisely

by staying in a close relationship

and contact with God.

I ain't playing craps

in the TV room all the time.

I'm tryin' to be productive

by writing these deeply felt

words that rhyme.

Getting it right with God,

so I can stay in line

going through all the changes,

Spiritual Lyrics

the process.

Man, oh man, I'm blessed,

because it could have been a lot worse,

but I don't have the time,

and besides it's a long story.

I give all the praise, honor, and glory

unto the Lord.

My prayer is, "Lord, please forgive my sins.

I'm sorry. Amen".

Others are ungrateful for coming into da cocoon.

complaining, straining, and explaining

why their urine is dirty.

Everything out of their mouths

is a curse word.

It's just absurd.

I wish I could invent something

that would make foul language

taste like a turd in someone's mouth.

These silly dudes catching cc's, dr's

and wanna-be rap stars in club bars.

Antonio Finn

Everybody professes to be your brother

or a Christian trying to tell ya

what's best while cross-dressin',

getting his groove on in the closet.

Having kids to raise,

you can't take care of them.

Going through that true-blue phase,

'cause another man is

taking care of your lady.

Baby, ya say it's crazy.

It could have been a lot worse.

They've been on the street with

an apple, crumb, or anything to eat.

You can't beat that.

In the beginning, I was

a worthless filthy worm.

Since I went through my long process,

I'm finally going home to be free

and take care of my son.

I can fly high in the sky.

Spiritual Lyrics

I'm a beautiful butterfly.

Amen.

Antonio Finn

12-21-04 GOD'S FULL ARMOR

Spiritual Lyrics

It's gotta be worn in the winter,

spring, fall, or summer.

You want to be very sharp

for when the enemy shows up

and not be dumb, dumb, and dumber.

You want to be able to stand.

You don't want to trip and become a tumbler.

Why not put on God's full armor?

First of all, here's what you have to do.

You must gird up your loins with the pure truth.

Yeah, ya gotta read it for yourself.

There's nothing wrong with confessin'

your sins to someone in a booth.

It may be all right for you,

but it's not goin' to get it for me.

I wonder what that smell was.

It kinda smells like metal bein' melted.

I guess God had it especially made for me,

and it's been welded together for me.

I'll give you a hint.

Antonio Finn

It's sort of like a hat you wear on your head,

and it's all wrapped up in salvation.

It's my helmet.

I want to tell you something,

and I know that everyone

has done this besides me.

Have you ever left your shoes off

and walked on the bare ground?

I know, just like me, you've felt that heat.

I got a trick for that this time.

I'm gonna cover my feet with the preparation

of the gospel of peace.

I have to protect my heart before it's too late.

Hey, I got this.

I'm always on top of things,

and I got it all covered up with my breastplate.

While I'm at it,

let me grab the shield of faith,

so that the enemy's darts

won't be able to faze me today,

Spiritual Lyrics

since I got what I need to protect my heart.

Those fiery darts won't be able

to penetrate through.

I know another thing.

I'm fed up with all of the devil's tricks.

As you can tell,

I'm very annoyed with him.

He must have forgotten that

I'm holding my sword of the spirit,

and I don't go anywhere alone.

What in the world is he thinkin'?

Doesn't he know that he'll be destroyed soon?

Let me hit 'im in his spinal cord.

That's if he even has one.

Devil, did you know that

me and God.

Ya should've tried to avoid us.

I'll wear it in the winter,

spring, fall, and summer.

I'm very wise and not dumber than I look.

Antonio Finn

I can stand now.

Yeah, that's right.

I'm not a tumbler anymore.

I feel so much better and calmer

than I was earlier,

'cause I've got on God's full armor.

Spiritual Lyrics

12-20-04 GOD IS GOOD

Antonio Finn

I'm often misjudged by people

who are in my neighborhood.

They think I'm a crazy person,

but I'm just misunderstood.

Beside all of that talk,

I'm glad that He's part of my life.

Jesus Christ died on the wood,

and I very loudly will share these words

to everyone who crosses my path

that God is good.

Even though things get kind of bad,

and things don't always go well daily,

I'll still bow my head low to the ground

with my head covered up with a spiritual veil.

I'll constantly praise God with my whole heart,

and send Him a sweet smell.

Saints, go ahead and open up your eyes,

so you won't miss your blessings.

You can see them now.

I don't really know

Spiritual Lyrics

how they're gonna come.

They might come through the TV.

or maybe through the mail.

Even though we don't deserve it,

You're still so good to us, God.

The many times when we did wrong,

You could have killed us.

Instead, you just spanked us

with your rod a little bit.

Do you want to know what's so odd?

You still find a way to bless us

by answerin' with a little nod.

You could have just told me no

for the many times

I asked for your help, Lord.

Thanks for helping me out

of all of my troubles.

If You hadn't helped me,

I probably would've selfishly

been mad about those things

Antonio Finn

that I desperately wanted

or the things I could've had.

You know, Lord, I still wouldn't

have justified my actions

for sometimes sayin' God is bad.

I guess I'm really tryin' to say,

You've always been good to me,

and no one else will I lean on.

Lord, You've been so good to me

even before I became a teen.

no matter what the situation,

You always found a way to intervene.

I'm often misjudged by the people

in my neighborhood.

they think I'm crazy,

but I believe I'm just misunderstood.

I'm so glad You're a big part of my life, Lord.

The one who died for all of our sins

on the old wood.

I'm also glad that

Spiritual Lyrics

I don't have to be upset anymore

about things that I should have had,

'cause You've already given me everything

I'll ever need.

God is good.

Antonio Finn

12-23-04 FOLLOW THROUGH AND FINISH

Spiritual Lyrics

I know that, at times, it gets mighty tough,

but I must keep on and follow through

with all of my dreams.

The things which I dearly long for,

and the very things I would like

to do in my life.

If You could have my eyes for a minute,

You'd see my dreams and goals.

I hope You enjoy the view.

Can You see me not stoppin' for anything?

Can You see me goin'

over and under obstacles?

I know without any doubt

that I'll make it, and with God it's possible.

As for me quitting,

that's out of the question,

and, for me, this isn't an option.

I hope I've made myself very clear,

or do you need a more logical explanation?

Well, here it is.

Antonio Finn

I must follow through

and finish what I've started,

'cause time is wastin',

and I gotta make it to my final destination.

I really don't have the time

to get held up from making progress,

so I think I'll skip all of the hesitation

and just keep on goin' forward.

I must be the one to say that

I fall down a lot on many occasions.

It doesn't stop me, though.

Really soon, I'll quickly dust myself off,

get up, and place a Band-Aid

on my abrasions, 'cause I know it

gets mighty tough.

I must keep goin' on and follow

through with all my dreams.

You know the things

I'd like to do in my life.

If You could just have

Spiritual Lyrics

my eyes for a minute,

You'd be able to see

all my dreams and goals,

so enjoy the view.

Please just try to picture me

going that extra mile.

That's a pretty long distance.

There aren't any quitters

in this field of work,

so it's gonna take much perseverance.

I'm gonna keep my eyes forward

Like I'm in His zone,

'cause I'm in a trance,

so why not with the Lord?

Shouldn't I take a chance?

I've done it with everything else,

but somewhere along the way,

I get a little scared and nervous

in this back-and-forth game of life

like I'm playin' a game of tennis.

Antonio Finn

Please, Lord, wipe out all my many sins,

so I can be whiter than snow,

and be without any blemish.

Your good servant can continue

to follow through and finish.

Spiritual Lyrics

12-18-04   FIRED UP AND DISGUSTED

Antonio Finn

Well, today, I'm havin' one of those days

where I'm fired up and disgusted.

I'm not feelin' too good,

'cause I'm broke, and my pockets

are really busted.

I don't know why the very things

and people I put my all into

always let me down,

No one can be trusted.

You should never sit around

waitin' for anything to just fall

from the sky into your lap.

Is there anyone to look out for me

like I've done for them?

You know the money handling.

Hey, it's all right though

'cause the Lord brought me this far

without your help.

All because of Him

I'm still standing.

Spiritual Lyrics

You can't keep a good person

down for long.

I refuse to stay down here

on this ol' ground,

but while I'm down here,

let me say a quick prayer

to the one who's

still the talk of the town.

Lord, please rescue me quickly,

And I wouldn't mind if You

do it right now.

If you can't come soon,

out of my mouth

You'd probably hear

a disgusting sound,

'cause I specialize in complaining

by turning an ant hill into a mountain.

I know I'm not the only one

over the entire globe

who's feelin' this way.

Antonio Finn

I'm so fired up

I'm burning a hole in my pocket.

Sometimes, I have to fake myself out.

I often play that role,

and I pretend everything is all right.

I'm gonna let the truth be told.

let me let you in on a little secret.

I'm really feelin' so disgusted and fired up

that I'm to just about to blow.

I've just gotten to the point

where I'm so sick of this type of life

and its ups and downs

that I want to just vomit sometimes.

The walls that around me

seem like they're closing in,

and I feel very sandwiched in.

I'm really tired of allowing

the fuse to be lit.

When I'm really under pressure, Lord,

can you do something for me?

Spiritual Lyrics

Please just fix it.

I need to get ready

to adjust to new changes in my life,

and I'm really tired of feeling this way,

'cause my pockets are busted.

The things and people

that I put my all into and trusted in

have failed me.

My faith in God has been

up on the shelf too long.

It needs to be dusted off.

Maybe then I won't feel this way anymore,

ya know, fired up and disgusted.

Antonio Finn

12-3-04 FAMILY SCAMMERS

Spiritual Lyrics

The very one you thought you could trust

has been tellin' you lies that you believed,

and they're not really concerned about us.

Have they been saying they don't think

you can do it all by yourself

and have the nerve to say for me

to help you out is a must?

They even try everything in the book

just to gain your surplus

and all of your possessions.

They wouldn't dare do it to a stranger

but only from flesh and blood family.

Ya know, the ones who you grew up with

and who raised you.

My brothers, sisters, uncle

and even my very own auntie.

God said it's the root of all evil.

Do you want to know what that is?

It's money.

It's not your fault if you're a victim

Antonio Finn

of family scammers.

Believe me, they make you want

to get in the flesh and choke 'em

or strike them with a hammer.

You can't do that

'cause you'd be actin' all ugly

just like you-know-who.

We should be practicing godly manners.

Please listen to me.

Just throw your hands up and give it to God.

They've really messed up now

'cause God and I are like two peas in a pod.

They'll get what they've been askin' for,

you know, the ones that commit fraud.

No one can save you

from the wrath of God's rod, you evildoer.

It's not that I'm glad

that this happened to you,

but you had me goin'

for a very long, endless ride.

Spiritual Lyrics

How can you hurt the one who loves you?

Do you even know about

the many nights I've cried?

That's all right 'cause God heard me,

and my cause is justified.

I see the expression on your face,

and you're lookin' so surprised.

Your eyes are bulging out of your head.

Why couldn't it have been a stranger,

Instead of me?

I've known you for so long.

For goodness sakes I'm your blood and family.

I didn't know you'd stoop so low.

Why did you act so desperately

for a piece of change.

It's only a small amount of currency.

Listen up, everybody,

you need to separate yourselves

from your family members who love to scam.

I wouldn't worry about it

Antonio Finn

if you've been victimized,

'cause God will always provide somethin' for you.

"Slam."

What's that that's caught up in the brushes?

Somewhere up in there lies a scam.

Spiritual Lyrics

11-22-04 EXPECT NOTHING BACK

Antonio Finn

This is for the kind souls

who are doing great works

for ungrateful people

and expect nothin' back.

All that hard work

you're doin' for someone else

and taking up their slack.

You can't even get a thank you.

Funny toward you they'll act.

They even have the nerve

to call you names and curse you out

by snappin' their fingers,

makin' their neck, head, and eyes swerve.

That kind of bad treatment,

I don't think anyone deserves.

That's all right.

Just say a quick prayer for them

and watch them bend a u-curve.

They'll definitely be comin' right back.

It's proven more than once

Spiritual Lyrics

I'm not just sayin' it.

It's a proven fact.

You can't expect nothin' back.

Man will let you down.

He won't even give you a thumbs-up

or no pitty pat on your back.

Why do people wonder why things

in their lives are goin' so out of whack?

I wonder if they ever thought

maybe it's something in their life

that they lack.

Please keep in mind

that anything back from 'em

you can't expect.

Guard yourselves from

feelings of rejection.

God will give you the confidence

that you need,

and He'll protect you.

Heed my words.

Antonio Finn

He'll make it to you direct.

Getting something back from Him

You definitely can expect.

If you expect somethin' back from man,

great will be the impact.

Whatever happened to that sayin',

If you scratch my back

I'll scratch yours?

Waiting on man will throw

all of your plans and everything

all out of whack instead of everything

being intact just like things should be.

From now on, don't expect nothin' back.

Spiritual Lyrics

12-12-04 EVICT HIM

Antonio Finn

Why was it my house

that you sought?

Creeping up slowly,

you weren't even detected.

You did it without bein' caught.

You started messin' with my mind

and fogging up my thoughts.

If you think you're gonna

continue to stay here, devil,

I think not.

I'm kickin' you out.

You're not my friend or acquaintance,

especially when you seduced one of Jesus'

disciples to trap Him with a tainted kiss.

Just look at this mess you made.

It's time for some of God's

high-powered maintenance.

If the devil tries to come back in,

I'll quickly evict him out.

I need to keep on the light of God

Spiritual Lyrics

on my porch and make sure

that the light doesn't go dim.

The devil will see that.

His chances of comin' back are slim.

Maybe that will keep him

in his own realm where he belongs

far away from me.

I'm really tryin' to stay

away from bad company.

Stinkin' devil, why are you lounging

around in my room?

Did you really think I'd let you

stay here another day?

That's what I assume.

Well, you were wrong,

so get away from me

as soon as possible.

I'll tell ya what.

There's a place made for you

among the tombs.

Antonio Finn

Why don't you go there, devil?

You'll fit right in with

all of the ghosts and goons.

Have I ever told you that

all those years you stayed with me,

you made a lousy tenant.

It never failed

how all of my money was gone,

'cause I was foolish with it.

Just look how I spent it.

You even influenced me

to get into trouble,

and I ended up not bein' the victim.

I was often the defendant.

I know now that you just were

watching and laughing at me

while I received my lengthy sentence.

Silly me.

Not once have you apologized

or entered into repentance unto God.

Spiritual Lyrics

That's all right,

'cause now you've been evicted.

You can't drive me anywhere anymore

'cause your license has been suspended.

You're just like a lost scout

wandering around in the forest.

I can hear you cryin'

loudly in a high-pitched voice,

singing a chorus.

Saints, go ahead and evict him

out of your lives.

Tell him to find

some other place to go stay.

Devil, don't even think

about comin' back here again.

Don't even look or come toward us.

Antonio Finn

12-11-04 DEAL WITH IT

Spiritual Lyrics

I want to know what I ever did to you.

Why the smart talk?

Was it something I said?

I don't think I deserve

to get chewed out.

I'm very sorry that I came by.

I just want some help,

but you didn't really care about me,

'cause you're too stuck on yourself.

To add a few more words

I believe you left your better attitude

at home on the shelf

instead of bringing it with you today

or is it just the way you are?

I guess I gotta just deal with it.

That's just how it is

in this day and age,

and You gotta deal with

people who are so wicked.

If you know what's best for you,

Antonio Finn

you need to get away from them

as far as you can,

and do it real quick.

I believe strongly in all

of the Lord's written commands,

which say, "Love thy neighbor as thyself."

Yes, people, it still stands to this day.

Somewhere along the way,

you must have missed it

with all of your silly ways and demands.

Do you think you're better than me

'cause you've got a little piece of land?

That still don't give you the right

to say those things to me.

It's not my fault you decided

to get out on the wrong side of the bed.

Your blanket is already unraveling

because of one little thread.

Do you know you could have

avoided this whole mess

Spiritual Lyrics

if you just had tightened up

or read your Bible?

You should've gone down

the straight and narrow road

instead of being misled by the devil.

I wonder why people act like that,

why they come off at us so mean.

I think they have

some issues with their self- esteem.

Why are they tryin' so hard

to make themselves

look bigger than You?

Inside they are so dirty

and not at all that clean.

It's just one their pipe dreams.

They're only fooling themselves

with that smoke screen.

Let it go up in smoke

right over your head.

I'm just bein' realistic.

Antonio Finn

They can drive you nuts

if you let them.

Some even had to go

to the hospital,

'cause they became very sick.

I'm not goin' to take all over their mess.

I'm gonna vomit.

I guess somewhere in their lives

they must have missed it.

Don't they know that life

is more wonderful than that?

Why must one act so stupid

toward other people?

Don't worry about it

or what they do to you,

'cause we'll be assisted by God,

and with His help,

we'll be able to deal with it.

Spiritual Lyrics

11-13-04 CARRY ME

Antonio Finn

I don't think that I can

go on any farther.

Can I get a helpin' hand,

my Heavenly Father?

The enemy is hot on my trail,

and it's me he wishes to slaughter.

I strive to give it to You,

Lord, at the altar.

Your hand is okay.

I need for You to carry me.

How can I bear my many problems?

They're about to bury me.

I'm sick and tired of the ridicule

and criticism that happens daily.

When they pick at me,

as if I were a cherry tree.

Lord, I can't cross the bridge of trials,

if the bridge is broken.

Please keep my mind,

heart, and eyes open,

Spiritual Lyrics

so that I don't fall in.

I can picture the enemy's face

bearin' a slow grin.

Today isn't the day. I don't want

to be soakin' or wet.

Lord, carry me.

Oh, thank You so much.

I'm now on dry land,

and this is where I want to be.

It's better than way up to here

with water way past my knees.

I can't believe this is happening to me.

I need to check somethin' really quick.

Hey, this is a real tree.

Because of the Lord,

I made it to the other side.

Things could've gotten a bit ugly

or I could've been caught up

in the tides of trouble.

I'm glad He came along with me

Antonio Finn

on this ride.

Lord, I'm also glad I stayed humble,

and I laid aside my pride.

Carry me, 'cause sometimes

I can't do it all on my own.

I'm not afraid to say that I need Thee,

and I occasionally get caught up

in my trials, sometimes daily.

I admit that I need to spend

more time with You,

so I can stay free.

Lord, please carry me

over these obstacles of life

which are many.

Carry me 'cause I'm really tryin'

to escape tragedy.

It scares me to think about burnin'

in the lake of fire

and bein' burned to the third degree

Oh, not me.

Spiritual Lyrics

Lord, carry me.

Antonio Finn

1-1-05   BUSY DOIN' WHAT

Spiritual Lyrics

Can you tell me what you're getting' done

and you're busy doing what?

You say you're takin' care

of your business,

but as far as I can see,

nothing has even been touched.

All of that lyin' you've been doin',

and you're only lyin'

to yourself, not to me.

You claim that everywhere you go,

they're givin' you the run-around.

You can't get any help.

You're just so heated

from all of the runnin' around

that you just melt.

Yeah, right.

Then tell me why you still spend

so much time enjoyin' yourself

by doin' everything from partying

to runnin' the streets?

Antonio Finn

How can anything good

come out of that?

In reality, it's full

of deception and deceit.

The devil is playin' you

like a puppet on a string.

Aren't you getting tired

of his defeat?

And he's just runnin' you ragged.

It's no wonder your body is so weak.

Check this out.

I know someone who can

fix it all right now.

If you haven't met Him yet,

it's about time that ya'll met.

There's something that you should know.

He's far greater than

anything or anyone,

and He's more important.

If you want to get on

Spiritual Lyrics

with your life

and get it together,

you need to obtain the promises

which He has for you.

They are your substances to keep.

It's all according to the Lord's ordinance.

Hopefully, the devil's works

don't mean anything to ya.

If I have convinced you

that the works of God make more sense,

handle your business.

Come on, people, let's get busy.

Maybe you're runnin around,

and you're doin' it without God's wisdom.

You're lookin' real silly,

and it's about time that you

get all your priorities straight

instead of runnin' around getting dizzy.

You say you're taking

care of your business,

Antonio Finn

but as far as I can see,

nothin' has even been touched.

The vines in your vineyard

are flowin' over in your life.

Do it quickly.

Someone needs to cut out that mess.

Oh, or are you just too busy?

Busy doin' what?

Spiritual Lyrics

AIN'T EASY BEIN' A CHRISTIAN

Antonio Finn

It ain't easy bein' a Christian.

Even though I made up my mind

and came to my decision.

I was sick of bein' bound up in prison.

I am so fed up with comin' in a room,

and all eyes are on you.

I can feel the haters' tension.

If they could,

when I turned my back,

they'd probably place a dart

under my ribs or in my lower parts.

They hated me right from the jump start.

This decision was one that shows,

for once in life, I'm smart.

I got sick of drivin' recklessly.

I finally decided to park.

It ain't easy then,

'cause the enemy

make plans for you.

He sees you as a target

Spiritual Lyrics

to bark up the wrong tree.

Don't worry.

He won't bite,

but he'll possess people

to provoke you to fight.

What if they actually hit you?

Should you turn the other cheek

or smile back?

It ain't easy to offer 'em a hand

that wants peace inside badly.

You want to roll up your sleeve,

put your Christianity down,

and give 'em a piece of your mind.

You can't do it, 'cause you know

you're a Christian.

Everything is recorded of you,

even our bad decisions.

The Lord put in us to do what's right.

Something within won't feel right,

as you lower your suspension.

Antonio Finn

You might have failed.

That's all right, saint, ask for

forgiveness or a gauge extension.

I know it ain't easy, of course.

It isn't always goin' to be all

sunshine and breezy when you get

turned again.

Shred 'em up with the Word

like the cheese on a pizza.

That's cheesy.

I know first-hand

it ain't easy bein' a Christian.

Can't tell if people are

serious or just playin'.

I'm always puttin' my guard up

like I'm on a mission, or I get mouthy

and say things I' don't mean.

Those aren't my intentions.

Excuse me, but I'm getting' this vision

that when we're tried by the enemy,

Spiritual Lyrics

he must first get God's permission.

Antonio Finn

11-30-04 BREAKTHROUGH

Spiritual Lyrics

I know you've been patiently

waiting for a breakthrough.

You've told yourself

to just give up.

You've been debating again,

haven't you?

This very time-consuming process

can be really aggravating.

When you don't get what you want,

then the next minute you're pleased.

The odds swing toward

the opposite direction.

What a tease life can be.

How can one be cured from this

dreaded wanting to give up disease?

Lord, help me to endure this pain please.

With Your power You can

Go ahead and release it on me.

There're so many people

Lookin' for a breakthrough

Antonio Finn

in some form or fashion.

You may need your bills paid

or maybe your marriage

is on the rocks.

Layin' down on the job

won't get it.

Just take action.

You need to just pray to God

from your heart,

and tell Him all of your needs

with sincere passion.

You also need to remove all doubt.

Then you can finally

get some satisfaction.

Go ahead and take out the trash.

Do a trash run.

Everything that's in your heart

and whatever you want answered,

don't be afraid to ask the don.

Before ya know it,

Spiritual Lyrics

your breakthrough will

be here in a while.

Go ahead and call Him up anytime.

Just pick up the phone.

Press the dial.

It's not going to be all fun and games,

'cause first you must endure the trials.

Sometimes you gotta get some

help from the house of prayer.

You may even need to go

that extra mile to seek His strength

by walkin' to the altar

and then down the aisle.

Saints, just sit back

and watch your troubles

all lift up off of you.

This is a warnin' to you.

Haters will hate your style,

'cause you're not worryin' like they are.

Remember that He has many things

Antonio Finn

for His child.

If we could just wait patiently

on your breakthrough, Lord,

we'd be fine.

If it hasn't come through for you yet,

the devil is hinderin' it,

but you can shake him loose.

Let him look all crazy

just like he's on Gray Goose.

Go on right ahead

and receive your breakthrough.

Spiritual Lyrics

12-30-04 RIDIN' THE STORM

Antonio Finn

As I look up in the sky,

I can see that it's getting dark.

The clouds are forming.

What am I goin' to do?

I gotta get it together.

There's no time for cryin' and moanin'.

Let me wipe my face

and just suck it up,

because it's comin',

so I best be getting ready.

I better grab a hold of God,

'cause the wind is pickin' up

kinda heavy.

Even though there's

some bad weather around,

I'm gonna still try my hardest

not to grumble.

Everybody has 'em

and must go through 'em.

I'm talking about trials.

Spiritual Lyrics

The key is to stay humble

and keep your eyes

open for dark clouds,

'cause you may hear a very loud rumble.

It ain't nothin' but lightning

and intimidating thunder.

You probably think you won't

make it through all of this mess.

You wonder.

These are just foolish thoughts

that you quite often ponder.

Don't worry about them

'cause that's just the devil

Tellin' you you're nothin' and a goner.

But you're not ridin' the storm alone.

You're ridin' it out with God.

Ride with honor.

You feel the wind pickin up,

and it's getting' kind of windy.

I don't know about you,

Antonio Finn

but as for me,

I'm gonna just dig my heels

in the ground with my cleats,

'cause up in the air isn't where I want to be

flyin' around up there

along with the debris.

As I look up in the sky,

I can see it's getting' dark.

The clouds are formin'.

What am I goin' to do now?

I gotta get it together,

'cause there's no time for cryin' and moanin'.

Some people may mistake

me for bein'' crazy,

They may laugh and scorn,

but I'm still gonna treat my storm

like a giant bull,

and take it by the horns.

I'm a man now.

Babies cry and mourn

Spiritual Lyrics

all day about their problems.

I'm goin' to dig my heels

 into that ol' bull's side.

Can you see me ridin' the storm?

Antonio Finn

1-6-05 MASTER CONDUCTOR

Spiritual Lyrics

Oh, God, thanks for

openin' up my eyes.

I can see this fine day,

and I know that trials will come.

I know somehow you'll

make them go away.

Sometimes I get so excited

when I talk, I spray.

If you're too close to me

when all of this is goin' on,

you may get wet.

Lord, I want to follow

after Your every step,

so lead the way.

You're a mighty good leader.

Of course, You are

the bread of life.

It's no wonder people were full.

Lord, You're the feeder.

At an early age,

Antonio Finn

You were about

Your father's business,

studying the word of God.

That's why You were

an excellent reader.

Drawin' crowds by the thousands,

You always spoke about Your father,

and You didn't care

about bein a people-pleaser.

May I add that You were a carpenter,

 and You really build people up.

I need to slow down

'cause I'm in the fast lane.

It's time for me to yield.

Don't ask me why.

I'm in the field of work

where one must learn

how to be still, watch carefully,

and pay very close attention

like orchestra members

Spiritual Lyrics

watch their conductor.

If I were you,

I'd link up with the Lord

who adds blessings to you

instead of followin' the devil

who's the reducer of blessings.

Lord, You're my favorite father

and the only master conductor.

Father, thanks for openin' my eyes,

so I can see this fine day.

I know trials will come my way,

but, somehow, You'll make

them go away.

Sometimes I get so excited,

When I talk, I spray.

If you're too close to me,

you just may get wet.

Antonio Finn

11-18-04   MAKING SOME PROGRESS

Spiritual Lyrics

I woke up this morning feeling good,

and last night I got plenty of rest.

I'm thankful to be alive.

May God continue to bless me.

It's time for me to make a move

and make some progress.

To succeed today is my goal.

I didn't get a chance to eat

even a bowl of cereal.

I'm goin' to see what the Lord

will allow to unfold for me.

I'm supposed to be in the

building at nine o clock.

I'm not worried about it,

'cause I know everything will be fine.

I'm goin' to get there early,

so that I'll be on time.

Lord I'm so glad that

you took the veil off from my eyes,

so I don't have to be walkin' blind.

Antonio Finn

I can see how it's going to work out.

I can finally see all of Your signs.

The counselor asked

everyone all of the questions,

and we all had a chance

to add our input in the discussion.

I don't know about everyone else,

but I've analyzed everything,

so I don't suffer any reductions

from my benefits.

To what the Lord has added

unto me already,

I guess there's no need for stress,

'cause my mind is already made up

for me to make some progress.

I didn't tell you how everything

worked out for me.

I killed two birds with one stone.

My counselor got

the information she needed.

Spiritual Lyrics

I got my copies at the touch of my phone.

Now that that's over,

these people gotta leave me alone.

They shouldn't have nothin'

to pick with me,

especially not a bone.

One foot forward,

and there's no lookin'

back on this quest.

Another one forward.

I know I'm truly blessed.

I don't have to guess,

and there'll be no complaining

from now on,

'cause I know I've done my very best.

God did what He promised me

and what He said He'd do.

I'm so impressed with Him.

For me to succeed

and have great success,

Antonio Finn

I need to let God walk

with me every day,

'cause it's time to

make some progress.

Spiritual Lyrics

12-15-04   LORD, THANKS AGAIN

Antonio Finn

I wake up in the morning

in a good mood,

and I pray for guidance.

That's how my days usually begin.

I'm really hoping that

today goes by very smoothly.

I guess it will all depend

on what will go on today.

How do I feel within?

I feel pretty good,

and if I hadn't said it before,

thank You for waking me up

this morning, Lord.

I had my eyes opened up wide

for something good to transpire.

Lately things have been

really tough on me,

and I've been tried in the fire.

I've been taking baby steps

and trying not to lose my footing,

Spiritual Lyrics

so I don't slip off the high wire.

At least that's what it seems like,

and the only peace and rest

I get seems to come at night.

Some people don't really have a clue

what I'm goin' through,

especially at twilight.

With so much cryin' and prayin'

with all your might,

I have to say thanks, Lord.

I know You saw I needed

a breakthrough.

My body couldn't afford

any more stress.

Lord, You had so much

sympathy toward me.

Thank you for the

blessings You gave me today,

all of those sweet rewards.

I thank you for all of the things

Antonio Finn

You do for me and my family.

Lord, how can I ever repay You?

I don't think any coupon

on earth could reduce my debt.

No rebate would help me out.

Lord, thanks for leading

me in the right direction

when I was blind and lost

heading right toward death.

Thanks for all of the times

I couldn't see straight,

and thanks for never failing me

and for being an on-time God.

You'll never be late.

Thank God I have so much more

to gain and less to lose.

Acknowledging You never slips my mind.

It's my choice to serve You,

and this is what I dearly,

from the bottom of my heart,

Spiritual Lyrics

choose to do.

There's no way

on Your green earth

that I could pay for all my dues.

I remember all the times I felt lonely.

Yes, Lord, You were a true friend,

and You wiped my slate clean,

cleaning up all of my many sins.

I can't think of any other man

that would have loved the wicked

even unto the very end.

Thanks for dying upon the cross.

I know that Your body rose back up again,

and in a cloud it did ascend.

I really do appreciate that, Lord.

Thanks again.

Antonio Finn

12-13-04   LORD, GIVE THE INCREASE

Spiritual Lyrics

I'm keepin' a watch out for

my blessing to see if it's coming.

Lord, Your Word says

if we ask for anything in Your name

we'll receive something.

I know I can count on You

and don't have any doubt

You'll keep Your word,

so my future looks promising.

You already know what's

needed from me before I even ask.

I wonder if You get upset with me

when the same request is repeated.

Please help me to forgive those

who abuse and mistreated

me in the past.

Lord, never let me act prideful

or get beside myself,

'cause I don't want to be

acting all conceited toward folks.

Antonio Finn

If You don't mind, Lord,

give me the increase

'cause the devil has my blessings.

My assets are frozen.

It's nothing for You, Lord,

to just roll up Your sleeves,

and I can see You'll soon be

wipin' out all of my problems.

Lord, You'll be using only

a little elbow grease.

Lord, I know that sometimes

I complain,

and doubt comes along

every now and then.

Just like a boat, I start

rocking and swayin'.

So help me stay on

the right track and the right lane.

I want to continue to obtain

my many blessings.

Spiritual Lyrics

What I really need to do

is break all of my bad habits.

My doubt is the main one

that I gotta cut out.

Maybe I could use a hatchet.

I've been doin' this so long,

it's become systematic to me now.

I've got to get this

straightened out now,

'cause I don't want none

of my blessings to go away.

I know God is very good

adding them up for me.

That's just God's mathematics.

I know without a doubt

that you'll come my way

and see about me.

For sure, Lord, you'll come through.

Sometimes I strain my mind

Tryin' to think of something

Antonio Finn

I can do about my problems.

All it does is stress me out.

It's almost like I'm about

to blow a fuse.

I thank God that you

add on to my blessings,

and you don't reduce any of 'em.

Lord, give me the increase,

and do whatever You want

to pour it out all over me.

Don't be shy, Lord.

Do as you please.

I understand it's at your pace.

Go ahead and release Your blessings.

I'm so thankful You give the increase,

and no one else does.

Spiritual Lyrics

LORD, BRING IT ON

Antonio Finn

I've been waitin' here

Tryin' to be patient,

but it's a little bit

too hard for me.

I'm still tryin' to be content.

I'm so used to having things my way.

With all of the contents,

Your power is potent and more.

Lord, bring it on.

Did You decide to lock the store?

I know You wouldn't

do that to me,

'cause You've

opened it up for me

many times before.

Lord, You said we're

the apple of Your eye.

As You can see,

I'm down to the core.

You promised to give me

Spiritual Lyrics

the desires of my heart.

When You give me

what I ask for,

I promise not to depart.

How could I do that to You

when You gave me

a brand-new start?

Lord, my sins, which are many,

You never mention.

I thank You for everything

that You do for me

and the extra attention.

I appreciate Your words.

How mighty are Your inventions.

Things are stackin' up.

Sometimes things happen so fast.

I often wonder if

I'm still getting punished

for old sins from my past.

No, that can't be right,

Antonio Finn

because one passage says,

"Our sins into the sea

You will cast."

Please, Lord, bring it on.

It seems like eternity.

I've been waiting for

an answer for so long,

the angels You sent

got caught up.

Could that be what's wrong?

'cause good and evil

are always battling each other

all of the time.

Angels are very strong.

Lord, I know I'm not the only one

who has a sad song.

Pour out Your blessing upon us, Lord.

Bring it on.

Spiritual Lyrics

12-17-04   LET'S WALK TOGETHER

Antonio Finn

Are you tired of strugglin'?

There's a way that things

can be better for you.

I know that it can be hard

goin' through the storm by yourself.

Life's stormy weather

can be very difficult.

I have a suggestion for you.

How about all of us

help each other out?

Let's all walk hand-in-hand together,

but first I must ask you

to keep a promise with me.

in all our situations,

we are gonna agree

to still be friends, all right?

Now that that's out of the way,

Let's start with your burdens.

You have a big pile.

Oh my, you got so many problems,

Spiritual Lyrics

it looks like we're gonna

be here for a while.

Let's see. Where do I start?

Where's the index or file cabinet?

That's okay with me

if we have a big mess ahead of us.

When I'm done with you,

vice versa things will soon

become versatile.

You see, if me and you both

help each other out,

we'll get farther ahead.

There'll be no more wet sheets

from our many tears wettin' the bed.

I'm to the point that

I'm fed up with the devil.

Do you know that

with God, we got the power

to walk all over

serpents and scorpion heads.

Antonio Finn

Down they'll go into

the ground we tread.

If we could just all learn

how to walk together,

we've won the battle,

'cause everybody

would be on their feet.

We'll make the devil so mad,

and we'd be gettin' things done.

If everybody in the world

would lift a hand to help someone,

then everybody wouldn't

have to struggle.

We'd all be helped, and I believe

we'll all get along with one another.

See, there's strength in numbers

'cause if one falls,

someone in the group will be able

to assist him/her whenever they call.

Let's be obedient

Spiritual Lyrics

to the Lord's commandments,

and that goes for all

of His strict laws.

One of them says,

"Bear each other's burdens,"

so go ahead and help

someone out of trouble

if you can

before it worsens for them.

Let's help each other,

and maybe we can break

all of the curses that are upon us.

I think the world would be

a much better place

for us all to live in.

Today let's help each other

through life's stormy weather.

Hey, let's walk together.

Antonio Finn

12-4-04 KEEP ON KEEPIN' ON

Spiritual Lyrics

Uh oh, I did it again.

I fell down flat on my face,

but I quickly got up off the

turf because of You, Lord.

I just got a taste plus in everything.

I'm learning to be abound and abase.

We must remain strong

and not get distracted.

No matter what,

keep up the pace.

I know the devil is throwin'

everything at you.

That's so you'll give up on God.

He wants to continue

to hold up your blessings.

Them he loves to prolong.

Suck it up, saints.

Keep on keepin' on.

Your eyes are lookin' forward

and forgettin' those things

Antonio Finn

which are behind.

The inspiration inside of me

says that I don't have

any longer to be deprived

of the very necessities

needed in my life.

I can survive, and

I'm gonna look unto the hill

whence my help comes from.

Let nothin' stop you

from receiving your ultimate prize.

Why wouldn't I keep on goin'

when the Lord has allowed me

to make it this far?

Unfortunately, along the way,

I've accumulated so many war scars,

everything from bein' abused

and friends walkin' out on me.

Lord I know ya see me cryin',

so collect my weary tears

Spiritual Lyrics

in Your jars.

I feel so much better

especially now that things

are stayin' up to par.

I can go ahead and proceed,

but I can't go anywhere

without my map,

'cause it'll be much needed,

and trouble might be close by.

What could you do

to protect yourself then?

If the enemy comes,

you couldn't do anything

'cause you're without your strap.

Remember that we're soldiers

in the Lord's army,

and we're fightin' for our lives.

We shouldn't let any obstacle

get in our way,

so keep up the forward progress.

Antonio Finn

It's our goal.

I advise that we're goin'

to keep our focus straight ahead,

and we're not goin'

to be lookin' side-to-side.

We'll make it to God, saints.

Finally, for once in your life,

you'll be satisfied.

You can make it

as long as you stay extremely strong.

Aren't you tired of being the devil's

and everybody else's pawn?

You need to treat

those ol' troubles that you have

just like they're dung.

Throw it all away,

and keep on keepin' on.

Spiritual Lyrics

12-5-04 JUST A TOUCH

Antonio Finn

Lord, Your manservant is feelin'

kind of restless tonight,

so, Lord, give me just a touch.

A dab will do it.

I don't know if I can take too much,

'cause the force of Your

glorious power makes my body jerk

and sometimes double clutch.

Today's word I could really use

a touch of Your power and healing.

You know, Lord, I'm trying

to reduce all these bad feelings.

I can't handle them all,

so I'll cast 'em on you.

Father, they'll become

Your dealings and not mine.

Lord, please take this fear

out of my belly.

It's way deep down inside my gut.

Can You just make

Spiritual Lyrics

a small incision in me?

Even though it may

hurt a little bit,

who cares?

It's just a little pain.

So what?

As long as You heal

my wounds completely up.

I won't fret about it,

'cause I know You'll make sure

that I'll get more

than the antidote.

I'll get the cure.

Lord, I can count on You,

'cause You're just that type of God.

You're not like man

who slacks your work.

God is very thorough.

All of the rest of my days

I shall be satisfied

Antonio Finn

'cause in God I must trust.

When things go wrong, Lord,

I'll try not to murmur and fuss.

I might not like it,

but I know it's for my own good.

Lord, please excuse all my complaining,

for I'm only dust.

Promise me this, Lord,

that You'll go down

and touch my innermost

deepest parts.

Lord, go into the chambers

where it's cold, black, and dark.

Gently clean the evil

and blackness from my heart.

I feel so drained,

so how about it, Lord?

I need a touch,

so I can get a quick jump start.

Whew, I really needed that.

Spiritual Lyrics

I feel so much better.

I feel like grabbin' a jump rope,

so I can play double Dutch.

I just can't keep this experience

to myself.

That's why I'm gonna tell

so and so and such and such

about it.

Lord, thanks again so very much.

All I needed from You was just a touch.

Antonio Finn

12-1-04 KEEP ME NEAR THE CROSS

Spiritual Lyrics

Sometimes I feel like

it's so hard to go on.

At times I feel confused and lost.

I'm askin' for You to

keep me near the cross.

I see myself as silver

in the melting pot.

My imperfections

cloud up the real me.

Lord, I need You

to take away the dross.

Hopefully, God will continue

to take care of me,

'cause He sees His Son's image.

I'm tryin' my hardest

just to make it there

until I can finish.

The ninety-nine just won't get it.

I'm gonna get a hundred percentage.

Lord, I understand why people

Antonio Finn

can't get along with me,

'cause I'm just a pilgrim

on my pilgrimage.

Lord, keep me near the cross.

Why do you have to deal

with lousy problems

from your boss?

Don't worry about it,

'cause he/she will soon

be on their way out in the cold

with their head numb from frost.

I guess now they'll realize

what they put you through.

Maybe they need to count up the cost.

I wonder if it came from

one of the oldest trees

which made the cross

that You had died on

for all of the world

and my iniquities.

Spiritual Lyrics

I don't know anyone

who would've taken those

penalties for me.

If I could make it to You,

maybe You'd wipe away

all of those painful memories.

It seems like every day

you must have some type of struggle.

Even if you mind your own business,

headed straight your way is trouble.

No matter how I try to avoid it,

it just seems as though

it multiplies into double trouble.

If I could get away

from it all, I would.

I'd take a quick trip

on a shuttle up outta here.

I wish I had a giant muzzle,

so I could wrap up

all of the world's trouble.

Antonio Finn

I truly believe I've said enough

and I sigh with much exhaustion.

I'm tired.

Come on, God,

please show the devil who's boss

and may I add,

Lord, keep me near the cross.

Spiritual Lyrics

1-14-05 I'VE JUST BEGUN

Antonio Finn

Hello, Lord. I know You'll

finish the work that has already

been started through me.

First, Lord, please pardon

all my iniquities.

It's kind of like how

the Red Sea was parted.

Since You've done this favor for me,

I'm ready to help the people

who are heavy-hearted.

I know that they really

don't know what to do

with their head hung low.

I'm here to tell them

that the Lord is good

for allowin' a closed door

to be swung wide open.

Isn't that wonderful?

You couldn't praise him enough

even if you had ten thousand tongues.

Spiritual Lyrics

Look out, world,

'cause here I come,

and I'm backed up by Almighty God.

Do you want to know somethin'?

I've just begun.

My sisters and brothers,

I beseech you that

I'm tryin' to lead you

to go and teach people

about the Lord Jesus Christ

to reach the ones who are weak.

I can hear some of you sayin',

"Here he goes again.

He wants to preach to me."

Well, I'm not goin' to do

what man says to do

but what God says to do.

He told me to go out

and teach the world.

Lord, may You empower me

Antonio Finn

to accomplish this goal

and give me more motivation.

Maybe I could reach people

through television and poems.

The ministry could be heard

all over the world.

If You'd bless me with a radio station,

maybe You could also send

some faithful helpers

who will sacrifice their time

and put their hearts into

everything that we do for You.

Yes, much dedication to You, Lord,

so I'll be able to help the heavy-hearted

with their heads hung low.

I'm here to let them know

that the door,

which was closed before,

the Lord will allow to be

swung back open.

Spiritual Lyrics

I don't think they'll be able

to thank Him

with ten thousand tongues.

Look out, world,

'cause here I come.

I just got started.

I've just begun.

Antonio Finn

11-21-04 IT'S IN THERE

Spiritual Lyrics

Everything we need

to walk daily and prepare

is in the Bible.

Just take time to read it.

I'm tellin' you, it's in there.

If you need strength to carry on,

and you feel like

throwin' in the towel.

Everything is goin' so wrong?

The Word helps us remain strong.

It helps a backslider

to come right back home

right where they belong.

Saints, you may have a miscarriage

or he/she just doesn't want

to comply in your marriage.

It's in there,

even if it's below average.

That's the way you're feelin',

and you can't keep up with the bills.

Antonio Finn

Don't worry about it.

It's no big deal.

My friend, open up the Word

if you want to know

the way of escape.

It shall reveal.

If we always use it

and stand on it,

the Lord promises

that your fate He'll seal.

If you need an answer

to your unanswered prayers,

the Lord has somethin' for that, too.

It's in there.

If you're feelin' lonely

like nobody cares,

I know exactly

what you're talkin' about

'cause I've been there.

The Word says we have a Helper,

Spiritual Lyrics

who's called the Spirit.

Give a holla up on high.

Go ahead and submit it.

It'll reach the heavens,

'cause it's transit.

Saints, listen to these

God-given lyrics.

Whatever you do,

don't take my word for it.

Read the Lord's holy word.

Read the Lord's transcript.

'cause it's in there.

There's also some protection

for those times.

When the enemy attacks you,

the Word has somethin' for him.

I believe you can read it

somewhere in the book of Acts.

It'll send him wherever he came from.

Yeah, with the swiftness

Antonio Finn

it'll send him right back.

Give him the old ax.

Tell me somethin'.

Do you easily scare?

The Word says to

send for some help

maybe a request or prayer.

Saints, we need to be more

active in the Word

bein' a doer not just a sayer,

'cause we're supposed to be

soldiers for the Lord

and demand slayers.

Don't worry about anything,

'cause there's something for that.

If you're not quite

up to God's standards,

the Bible could help

you with that problem.

No matter what

Spiritual Lyrics

the problem is, it's in there.

Antonio Finn

12-27-04 IT'S ALWAYS SOMETHIN'

Spiritual Lyrics

Oh, my God, here we go again.

There ain't nothin'

that irritates me more

than troubles

I try my best to avoid.

I don't know why,

but it always seems

to get under my skin.

It seems like when I struggle

through one problem,

from out of nowhere

comes more trouble

that I can't handle.

Come on, Lord,

let's make a big play now,

'cause the play clock

is counting down fast.

Let's break out of the huddle,

'cause, Lord, at times,

this body wants to just give up.

Antonio Finn

Yes, it gets very weak.

I admit that almost all the time

I need your help.

My burdens are heavier than concrete.

Why is it that

every time I turn around

It's always somethin'.

It'll be nice

if I had a little company

while I'm goin' through my trials.

Unfortunately, I don't think

there's anybody comin'.

I know the Lord will.

I thank God you're always present,

and it's you I'll always be wantin'.

I guess I just have to face facts.

From people I should

expect nothin' back.

I'm just sittin' here stuck

with all of my troubles

Spiritual Lyrics

and all of my problems.

Some people are just more

concerned about themselves.

They don't want to get involved

with your big mess.

I should've known better

than think they'd probably

help me out.

Foolish me.

Why did I think that

when they don't even call.

I guess they're all left

for me to solve on my own.

Oh, my God, here we go again.

There ain't nothin' that

irritates me more than troubles

I try my best to avoid.

I don't know why,

but it always seems

to get under my skin.

Antonio Finn

God, I know you see and

know everything that

I go through,

'cause you're a true friend.

Lord, I refuse to go crazy

and end up in a looney bin,

'cause life may do that

to some people.

Lord, why do I have to go

through these trials?

Why is it always somethin'?

Spiritual Lyrics

11-23-04 INNER BEAUTY

Antonio Finn

Some people are so quick

to judge people by their

good looks or appearance.

They should be more concerned

about their sins and

praying for God's deliverance.

Instead they make people feel bad.

Saints, I know it's painful

to endure these things.

You need to keep goin' on

with God's endurance.

You're precious to God,

for we're all His servants.

Please remember that

patience worketh perseverance,

and we must remain strong,

so souls can be saved.

It's our obligation and duty.

If you never heard

these words before,

Spiritual Lyrics

you're hearin' them now.

I'm sayin' you have God's inner beauty.

So what if people don't like

your body or your face?

Just remember you have

the beauty of God's grace.

You need to forget about

those uneasy feelings.

Just ask God to erase them.

If you want some real beauty,

His steps you must constantly trace.

Hey, all you wicked people.

Why do ya act so ugly?

They also use this word

to describe someone's looks.

If someone looks pudgy,

they may not have

a cola bottle shape

with everything

stickin' out and bulging.

Antonio Finn

So what?

To God you're beautiful anyway,

and you're not ugly.

True beauty is not outward.

It's from a person's inner core.

It's not based according to

how they look in the face

or being a little bit thinner.

They're just jealous,

'cause you're the real winner.

You should have more

confidence in yourself than that.

You're not a beginner

like you used to be.

Think on these good things,

sunsets. roses, heaven, and

God the almighty creator

and the Lord God our king.

He made all human beings.

You should know for a fact

Spiritual Lyrics

that you have His inner beauty.

Instead of wanting to hear,

"Hey, Cutie."

It doesn't matter

about all of that junk.

What's my main point?

It is to have God's

true inner beauty.

Antonio Finn

12-28-04 IRON SHARPENETH IRON

Spiritual Lyrics

I finally got tired of

bein' disobedient unto God

and also of bein'

a knucklehead and numbskull.

I used to act like I didn't have

nothin' up there in the hull,

but one day I decided

I had enough of bein' so dull.

The Lord touched my soul,

and then I knew I wanted

a brand-new start,

like the pointed end of a dart.

As you can tell by now

I want to be very sharp

'cause you know that

iron sharpeneth iron.

Lord, I can't do it by myself.

It gets a little bit

rough and very tiresome.

Lord, sharpen me up like

Antonio Finn

the horns on the mighty bison.

I want to be as sharp

as the stars in the sky

that shine on a dark night

on the belt of Orion.

Can anybody understand my words?

Can you relate,

or with your conscience

do you debate?

I'm no longer dull and raggedy,

but now I'm so straight

cuttin' through my enemies

like a razor blade.

This is how we gonna do it.

When one is dull,

we need to sharpen the

other one.

Whoever it may be,

let's read the word,

My sisters and my brothers,

Spiritual Lyrics

at times you may think

you can make it by yourself,

but when it all comes down to it,

we do really need one another.

If this sayin' wasn't true,

the Lord wouldn't have said it.

Besides, I discovered it

in the Lord's word.

Listen to me.

I finally got tired of

bein' disobedient unto God and

bein a knucklehead and a numbskull.

I used to act like I didn't

have nothin' up there in the hull,

but one day I decided

I had enough of bein' dull.

At times, it gets rough

and quite tiresome.

Lord, sharpen me up like

the horns on the mighty strong bison.

Antonio Finn

Lord, I want to be as sharp as

the stars in the sky

on a dark night

on the belt of Orion.

Finally, I'm sharp,

so I'll help someone else

who's dull and knows

for a fact that iron

sharpeneth iron.

Spiritual Lyrics

IGNITE ME (11-14-04)

Antonio Finn

Come on, Lord, do something

To excite me.

I don't know if it's

around the corner.

Hey, it might be.

Go ahead, Lord, I'm

quite ready to be struck.

Heavenly Father, ignite me.

Whenever You're ready, Lord.

You can start before

I do anything.

Say a few words,

so my sin can depart.

Add fuel to the inner parts

of this sometimes

wicked, achin' heart.

How awesome and great Thou art.

Trigger the very things

that should be right in me.

It's so exciting.

Spiritual Lyrics

Bring out Your touching torch.

Yes, Lord, ignite me,

so I can be used mightily,

so my career can take off.

Promise Your servant that

he won't burn out

like old coal left

in the cold to cool,

or like an old, worthless,

worked-down old mule.

Lord God, You know my heart thoughts.

To serve You is my desire.

Don't let me turn away like others.

I don't want to become tired.

Allow me to continue to be inspired.

Oh, Lord, You ignite me.

You lit the fuse

that's shining so brightly.

As long as I stay in the light,

it won't go out.

Antonio Finn

Most likely keep me burnin',

'cause I know some won't

respect what I say.

Some don't like me.

If they do something to

Your manservant, my Lord,

I know You won't take it lightly.

Down comes the thunder and lightning.

Don't act all scared.

After all, the Lord

can be frightening.

I'm gonna keep it real

and stay right.

It's time to take off,

so I can take my flight.

come on in, Lord,

so You can light me

as well as ignite me.

Spiritual Lyrics

12-24-04 I'M NOTHING WITHOUT YOU

Antonio Finn

Ya know, Lord,

I'm nothin' without you.

Lord, I wouldn't be here today,

and I wouldn't have my being.

Who can feel what I'm rappin' about?

With me now many

people are agreeing.

Lord, I can't see all that well.

Your vision is made

just for seeing

afar off and ahead.

You're the only one

who comforts me in

the middle of the storm

and after.

I'm done weeping.

I gotta remind myself

that I'm nothin' without You.

I don't even think that

in my time of trials

Spiritual Lyrics

I could've made it through.

How could I have kept on

goin' by myself.

My salvation and dreams

would I have even pursued.

What is the reason

for havin' a machine

without havin' the screws?

It just wouldn't work.

Lord, without you,

how could I proudly

walk down the street

full of perk?

I'm gonna milk this moment

for all that it's worth,

'cause no one can

put me down anymore.

I refuse to go down

to the earth.

I wouldn't be able

Antonio Finn

to heal completely

from all of those years

of pain and so much hurt.

I'm not goin to lie.

Sometimes I take credit

for things that You do, Lord.

It's nothin but my selfish pride.

Antonio needs to just stop it.

Lord, without You,

no one on earth

would even be alive.

Without You, Lord,

I wouldn't be able to stand

whenever trials come.

If You weren't there for me

I'd probably just leave.

I wouldn't even wake up.

I'd still be restin'

and sound asleep.

Lord, without Your air,

Spiritual Lyrics

this temple and these organs

wouldn't be able to breathe.

I wouldn't even be here

or not have my being.

Who can feel

what I'm rappin' about

and with me how many

people are agreeing?

Lord, I can't see all

that well or that far.

Your vision is made especially

just for seeing far.

I know just what I need to do.

Say with a loud voice

He gets all the credit

from now on.

Thank You, Lord, for allowin'

me to be able to make it

through all of these trials.

Saints, this sayin'

Antonio Finn

is all so real and so true.

Lord, I'm nothin' without You.

Spiritual Lyrics

12-30-04   I'M EVER SO SORRY

Antonio Finn

I wondered what happened to me

when I acted like I did that day,

and why she didn't listen

to the words I had to say.

I knew I couldn't look after you.

My answer should've stayed nay.

Somehow, I said yes

and I still was convinced

to look after you despite

the pain in my back

just like I fell down

and landed on a fence.

You were such a good person,

and whenever I said, "Do this,"

You'd do it,

When I said, "Come here,"

you came.

The bad thing about it

is you couldn't even protect yourself.

You put up no defense.

Spiritual Lyrics

I just can't understand

why it happened to me.

It still doesn't make any sense

why it happened to you and me.

To this day, it still is

a touchy subject.

It still very much bothers me.

Can you please in some way

accept my apology?

I'm ever so sorry.

Why did it happen when

you gave me so much love?

When I was feelin' down,

You gave me many hugs.

I accept what I've done.

I'm not goin' to blame it

on the alcohol and drugs.

I treated you

like you were a throw rug.

I should've gotten some help,

Antonio Finn

'cause I had to be sick in the head.

I couldn't forgive myself.

For about three years,

I wished I was dead

for doin' that to you,

'cause you could've

permanently gone to bed.

I guess everything

does happen for a reason.

Through this experience

I now know that, Lord.

I even read the daily bread.

If I could just set back

the hands of time,

I would change everything

at the drop of a dime.

But then maybe I

wouldn't have become saved.

I could have been dead,

and I wouldn't have

Spiritual Lyrics

written these rhymes.

I pray to God that

you'll forgive me

maybe in this lifetime.

What happened that day

will never happen again.

I can't put anyone

through that kind of pain

no more, my friend.

I don't think people

know what I've gone through

or where I've been.

I wouldn't wish that

on my worst enemy,

so don't wish it on ol' Finn.

I know I should've just fessed up,

and I shouldn't have lied,

but I was so scared.

Man, you almost weren't here.

You almost died.

Antonio Finn

The Lord saw I didn't mean it,

and He saw me whenever I cried

with all garbage laid aside.

I think, God, that

you turned out just fine.

Believe me I had what I deserved.

Day for day I got mine.

I mean every word.

I write from my heart,

word for word and line by line.

I know what happened that day.

I didn't know the Lord back then,

so you know I didn't pray.

I was full of the devil,

and I slipped from

following the truth.

I strayed away,

and this was one of

my biggest mistakes.

Believe me it was enough

Spiritual Lyrics

to get my attention,

and it was more than

enough to shake me up.

At one time,

I didn't care about people.

I took pleasure

in hurtin' people,

but now I'm wide awake.

Thank you, Lord,

for forgiving me

for all of my sins

and savin' Your servant

from the fiery lake.

Lord, I don't want to ever

go through that again.

Lord, keep me from causing

pain to anyone else anymore.

No pain or agony.

Lord, You knew for years

that this sin bothered me.

Antonio Finn

Right now, Lord, I want to sign

a spiritual decree.

Lord, please pray for me

that I never do this again.

This is dedicated to the one

I afflicted a long time ago.

Please accept my apology

from the bottom of my heart.

I'm ever so sorry.

Spiritual Lyrics

1-1-05   HAPPY NEW YEAR

Antonio Finn

My God, I finally made it,

and it's all because of You.

I can't believe another year is here,

and I made it through.

Last year was so hard for me.

Now the Lord is bringin' in the new.

Loud screams are all I hear,

and some people believe

it's just fun and games,

so they pop beers.

Some saints somewhere,

in a church or at home,

maybe are sheddin' some tears.

They wanted to give up,

so that's why God stepped in

and kept them on the right road.

God bless ya'

'cause you didn't veer off the road.

I want to wish you a happy new year.

Do you want to know my resolution?

Spiritual Lyrics

All right, here it goes.

It's to get a little closer

than I was last year to God.

I have to bind all of

the devil's confusion sometimes,

and I'm gonna make sure

the chains are completely off

and not just loosened.

It's about time for

a new revolution this year.

I'm not goin to just settle

for patchin' things up.

I'm goin' for the curin' solution.

I've got somethin' to talk about,

and somethin' to really celebrate.

I'm alive and well.

The Lord has me pretty much protected,

and that's according to my great faith.

I know I'm not alone here

and someone else can relate.

Antonio Finn

Before I forget.

It's okay if you want

to watch your weight.

Keep this in mind.

You really need to know

the man who can

get you in the gate.

The reason why I talk like this

is because God

is hardly talked about.

He's the real reason

why you're seein' another one.

It's not a big ol' party.

You have it all confused

with a Mardi Gras.

I'm quite sorry you had

a hearty pill to swallow.

My God, we made it,

and it's all because of You.

I can't believe that it's another year,

Spiritual Lyrics

and we made it through,

'cause last year was

so hard for us all.

Now the Lord is bringin' in the new,

and loud screams are all I hear.

Some people really believe

it's just fun and games,

so they just pop beers.

Some saints somewhere

are sheddin' tears.

They wanted to give up,

so God stepped in and kept them

on the right road.

God bless ya',

'cause you didn't veer off the road.

Now that's somethin' to cheer about.

Happy new year.

Antonio Finn

(7-6-02) HOPE

Spiritual Lyrics

Today isn't like an average day.

I'm thinking about hope.

Everybody has it

even that ol' crackhead

who steps to cop dope.

It can also be false,

so don't expect to find it

in the so-called pope.

You can see the eagerness

in a baby's eyes

searching for Mama's breast.

As I happily go walking

down the street to the store

without getting shot,

someone is about to

face the judge

or be charged with murder.

Can ya' imagine the stress?

You just done ecstasy

and had multiple sex partners.

Antonio Finn

Now you think you caught AIDS.

Kelly just took her exam

to get her master's degree.

Did she get a good grade?

You've been doing a good job

at work.

Will your salary get raised?

Lord, how much longer

must I suffer?

My motion is in.

When will I get relief?

They keep dragging us

with everything.

When we call home,

they're in disbelief.

They think we're just overreacting.

Good grief.

You dial "1",

then your pin number,

then the number.

Spiritual Lyrics

It says it's invalid.

Frustrated as you are,

you try again.

No answer.

Man, I'm tired of this.

I want to go home.

Someone just tried you.

Oh, no he didn't.

Oh, yes he did.

The authorities talk to you

like you're a dog.

How very rude.

How convenient it is for them

to take it out on us,

because of last night's family feud.

Lord, forgive them

for they know not what they do.

Ignorant, foolish, and idiotic people.

Excuse me,

but it's time for a brotha'

Antonio Finn

to get knee deep,

because those things

which exalt themselves

against God won't prosper,

and they'll soon reap,

so what are you waiting for?

Get on your knees

and petition the Lord.

Now you can get some sleep,

you hope to see another day.

You could have been cut off from

getting a visit from your family

and hearing them say,

"We love and miss you,"

or receiving a reduction

of your sentence,

being able to discern

between right and wrong,

or hearing words of encouragement

from your brothers

Spiritual Lyrics

saying that you grew.

Hope is seein' your kids for

the very first time in years.

Hope is when you get a letter

from your spirit-filled

mom or grandma which reads,

"God loves you. So do I.

We're all doing fine."

Hope is knowing,

after all of this pain and suffering,

there's a better life.

When our Savior took that

big step for us all.

Imagine Him on the cross,

drained, exhausted from

multiple beatings,

blood pouring out His back

and trickling down His face.

Thorns pressed and beaten in His skull.

What tremendous pain

Antonio Finn

when they speared Him in His side.

Out came the blood and water.

For His blood,

you're cleansed of your sins.

The water represents purity.

You must go down

in the water in Jesus' name,

so you can see Him

and be born of His spirit.

Finally, He whispered these three words,

"It is finished," with His head hung low.

Our Savior gave us hope.

I have hope.

You have hope.

People, we all have hope.

Amen.

Spiritual Lyrics

HE KEPT ME FROM FALLIN'

Antonio Finn

I open up my eyes to collect myself.

Aw, man, I'm still in here.

Oh well, I still have my health.

Not all that wealthy in here,

but I don't need no wealth.

Whoops, almost forgot to pray.

I must get prepared today.

I guess I should be on my way

to see what the Lord

has for me this day.

How can two walk together

unless they agree?

Lord, I'm blessed

'cause of Your amazing grace.

Some like a hot taste

and ain't met toothbrush and paste.

Probably, some didn't wash their face.

I can't stomach this food.

Others have it gone without a trace.

It's time to go up to the gate

Spiritual Lyrics

when they call your name.

Ya' better not be late.

If you are, carry your own weight,

'cause I've got mine.

This here is my time.

Wish I could press rewind.

I'd do it at the drop of a dime.

Uh oh, I heard my name.

It's time for me to face the pain.

He's putting me down.

Hey, man, watch the frame.

There I go out the door.

I'm hearin' that boy's mighty poor.

What he's sayin'

a small voice in my head says, "ignore."

I arrive in a van,

and throw my lunch bag

on the floor.

I'm thinkin' about diggin' ditches

working for free

Antonio Finn

while investors count their riches.

I'm on the highway

around tall bushes

making my way to the street.

A car just missed me by inches.

"Oh, thank God," I prayed.

It's not worth it

'cause we work for free.

I'll be glad when this is over.

This isn't where I want to be.

They got me pickin' up trash

and sweepin' the street.

Oh, my God, the ground

has gone from under my feet.

This can't be happening to me.

What about my son and family?

Maybe my mind is full of deceit.

There is no need for stallin'.

The guys come over

from across the street.

Spiritual Lyrics

They're laughin'

while I keep crawling.

It's a long way down,

so I pulled myself up to the ground.

He kept me from fallin'.

It's hard to fight back my tears

and keep from bawlin'.

I just received a letter

from my Christian mother, Cathy.

It read, "He's able to keep

you from fallin'."

Antonio Finn

HANDLE MY BUSINESS

Spiritual Lyrics

It's all up to me.

I'm not gonna hold my breath

and wait around for nobody.

When you're seeking help,

where's ya' friends or family?

If ya' really want the truth,

they can barely take care of themselves.

I've been independent from my youth,

so how can they assist me or you,

so they're off of my list?

I guess those ol' problems

have been dismissed.

It's better to handle my business.

Can anybody get anything right?

That's something you gotta do yourself.

May I add don't let your right hand

know what you're doin' with the left.

Some of you men

are wearin' something else.

I guess most of the women

Antonio Finn

are wearin' the pants and the belt.

I know some of you

may be a little bit mad at me.

Take it up with God Almighty.

It is in His decree.

Down the ball and take a knee.

No need to get knee-deep,

'cause depths pile up.

They crawl and creep.

If I had handled my business

in the first place,

this wouldn't have happened.

I wouldn't have to weep.

God said, "That's what you get.

Instead of listening to me,

I guess you guys will

just cry together."

Who can handle

it better than you?

Definitely not your family or crew,

Spiritual Lyrics

'cause everything I let them handle,

they always blew.

You need to tie your own shoe,

and I must confess

I'm sick and tired of bein' tried.

My stress level is up.

Man, I gotta watch it.

Why should I be in distress?

May I add a few more words

nothin' more and nothin' less.

May God bless.

I don't have anyone

to help me out of this mess

beside God and my wife.

I really need to handle my business.

Antonio Finn

ARE YOU READY?

Spiritual Lyrics

One of these days the world

will be in mayhem.

People will be disappearing

right off the face of the earth.

Oh, won't that be grim?

Many people will be

searching high and low for

their loved ones

all around the earth.

They'll call the missing person's hotline

and paying whatever it's worth.

Oh, my God, a child's mother

has just disappeared

right out of the crowd.

Will someone please help

comfort that child

for cryin' out loud?

Her mother has gone

up in the clouds.

Planes crash, cars swerve

Antonio Finn

out of control,

and people are rioting.

An oil truck has just

flipped over on its side and spilled.

Can anybody make any sense

out of this?

Can anyone heal?

My God, someone just got killed.

Many will try to seek

assistance from the church,

'cause we know the true answer.

In a small town,

Maria just set little Timmy

down on the dresser.

When she turned around,

all she saw was his shoes and clothes.

She started to cry helplessly

running down the road,

She asked everyone

if they saw her son,

Spiritual Lyrics

but no one did.

Peter calls for his wife, Jina,

but there's no response.

He checked the bedroom

and only found her purse,

shoes, clothes and a letter.

It read, "Dear, I'm with the Lord.

Please seek the Lord

and look after the kids.

Love you, Jina."

He wishes he had treated

her a little better.

Some people will be partying,

drinkin', and boogyin' down,

or just plain out gettin' drunk.

Leon sees a foxy chick

and approaches her to ask

for her number or a dance.

Right before his eyes,

she vanishes.

Antonio Finn

Maybe he's just too drunk.

The government officials

will be giving speeches

advisin' people to stay calm and not panic.

In reality, you'll have

every right to get prepared.

Joe just can't take it anymore.

He's very frantic.

I encourage whomever

may be missin' loved ones,

please don't cry, weep, or worry,

because they made it

into the kingdom of heaven.

Glorious glory.

I would like to be with them, too

in a heartbeat and a hurry.

Up there with your Maker

livin' for eternity.

The question is

are you ready?

Spiritual Lyrics

WHO ELSE BUT YOU

Antonio Finn

Lord, in a little while

we gotta move

all because an in-law

didn't pay or do what was right.

She played around

and didn't pay bills

that were due.

My Lord, I'm sitting

around stressin' daily

tryin' so hard to figure out

where we can get some help

or relief from who?

I haven't got a clue.

It seems the longer I wait

time is winding down.

It's me and my ladybug

takin' turns scratchin' our heads

and sayin', "There's no one

to be found around."

Then we were told

Spiritual Lyrics

we'd soon have some relief

from some potential buyers.

Those silly clowns backed

out of the deal.

You can't always go

by what sounds good.

No matter what happens,

let's keep our faith in God,

to Him cry aloud.

He sees we're really tryin'

to do our very best,

so we're makin' Him proud.

Don't worry.

We're gonna make it through

by liftin' our many prayers

up through the dark clouds.

I don't think the Lord

will allow us to forget

that at one point in our lives,

we were stuck in the miry clay, the muck.

Antonio Finn

We couldn't find our way

out of the ongoing rut.

The storm and whirlwind of trouble

spun us 'round and 'round

in that same rut.

We didn't know who

would do it for us, but You.

When we didn't know

here we were gonna live,

You blessed us with this

little cozy place in our view.

This came from no one else.

Those blessings came from

no one but You.

They weren't by chance or good luck.

Lord, if You want to,

You could just stop there,

but You didn't.

Thanks for allowin' us a mover's truck.

Before You blessed my wife,

Spiritual Lyrics

she all night often sobbed

slavin' for pennies

and livin' paycheck-to-paycheck.

Boy, was she getting robbed.

I thank God,

and I'm so happy to hear

there's more bread on the table

and more butter for the corn on the cob.

I remember when people

were acting funny

sayin' that we probably couldn't make it

without that extra golden honey.

It finally arrived

through the hurricane crisis funds.

Lord, thanks for the extra money.

In a little while, I gotta move

'cause an in-law didn't

do what was right

and didn't pay what was due.

I'm just sittin' around stressin',

Antonio Finn

tryin' to figure out

where we can get some help.

I haven't got a clue.

Me and my wife needed about $1,000

to get into our little place.

We didn't know where we'd get

that kind of money from

or who'd do it for us.

It came from out of nowhere.

It came from out of the blue

from who else, Lord, but You!

Spiritual Lyrics

FAREWELL, FRIEND

Antonio Finn

You were my best friend's

oldest brother.

You did everything

to take care of your people,

includin' your dear old mother.

You were so cool in every way.

A special friend indeed,

so why ask for another man?

You were like my role model.

I tried to copy those

things you did.

I wanted your steps to follow,

sharing a bottle

by takin' one or two swallows.

My friend, the girls to you

weren't much of nothin'

like flies to food nothin'.

You had those good looks,

and you could blow all those notes.

Boy, you could really sing.

Spiritual Lyrics

I could tell that in your life

you wanted to change.

I tried to tell ya about

that no-good chick.

I heard of love at first sight,

but hookin' up with her

was too quick,

especially with all her lies.

You still fell hard!

She had many tricks.

My friend, I wished you

would've thrown in the towel

and called it quits.

We used to have so much fun

goin' to the mall.

Man, it hurt my heart

to tell ya what your wife had done.

For a split second, I thought

I had to take off and run,

but you just stood there

Antonio Finn

lookin' dazed and stunned.

My homeboy said

you went out and bought a gun.

He said you were actin' and

talkin' foolish and crazy

sayin' you wanted

to end your life

over this wretched lady.

Man, I said you couldn't trust her,

especially when she gave me her phone number

and called me "baby."

When a woman spends the night

at her ex-boyfriend's house,

something is seriously going on!

You just gestured to me,

"Yeah, maybe."

I remember in 1996 around December

you couldn't take it anymore.

You took the gun and shot yourself,

ending it all.

Spiritual Lyrics

Down you went like timber.

I felt a bad spirit in my soul,

so I called.

When my friend answered,

all I heard was an awful wail.

You probably would still be here

if you had gotten help.

Life's hell.

Maybe you could've gotten help

in hospital or in a cell.

Another precious talented life gone.

I miss you, Friend.

Farewell.

Antonio Finn

A FATHER TO THE FATHERLESS

Spiritual Lyrics

I lost my father at an early age.

Oh yes, it was tragic.

After it happened,

my mom lost her mind

so fast like an automatic.

Can anybody feel what I'm goin' through?

I wish I could straighten it all up,

"poof" like magic.

It ain't happening.

I don't care 'cause to me, Mom,

you're still a queen.

Much love to you.

Father, to me, you're still my king.

I'm so sorry that ya'll

didn't get to tie the knot.

Dad, you getting on one knee with the ring.

You know, having fun

and accomplishing things.

Dad, I have some faint memories of you.

I remember how you spoiled

Antonio Finn

me and my sisters with lots.

It didn't matter to us

where you got it from

or where it was bought.

Father, growing up without you

was hell and so tough.

At times, the road still gets a little rough.

I must face the big fish

and get swallowed up.

I sit for a while until I've learned my lesson.

Then I finally cry out,

"Lord, I've had enough."

I remember it well.

Where shall I begin?

It was show-and-tell day,

and I was feeling sad

'cause all the kids' dads were comin' in.

Man, was it eatin' me up inside.

"Finn," the teacher called.

I nervously put on a fake grin.

Spiritual Lyrics

Oh, my God, it's happening again.

Now I am mad.

How can I possibly compete

with all of these dads?

I finally pulled myself together

and showed the only thing I had.

It was a picture.

The class started clapping.

I made it through it.

It wasn't all that bad.

Hey, Dad,

I heard stories

about you at the age of fourteen.

You soared out, stayin' on your own.

I miss you so much.

It seems like I've cried my eyes out enough.

Man, I done poured out.

I know everything will be all right,

especially if the Lord

pulls this board out.

Antonio Finn

I heard that you knew martial arts

and about your man bouts.

I don't care what I heard

concerning you, Dad.

You just got caught up

goin' the wrong route.

I still believe you were a great person,

       and that's no doubt.

If you were still here,

I would've done a little more thinkin',

and, probably wouldn't have done

the smoking and drinking.

I wouldn't have been doing

those stupid things that

started my life sinking.

You would have gotten a hold of me

and done the neck wringing.

Like a bird, I been down

the loud singing.

Blockin' and weavin'

Spiritual Lyrics

'cause of all of your hand swingin'.

I turned out pretty good, Dad.

From heaven you can see.

I'm a brand-new man

and a fresh dad out pretty good.

If you can see the change,

don't you think less sometimes.

I have stress,

but I have a Heavenly Father.

I really need to love Him more.

Dad, He's over you,

no disrespect.

I hope that you'll understand.

Dad, God blesses never too little,

but nevertheless,

nothin' more and nothin' less.

Jesus Christ is to all

a father to the fatherless!

Antonio Finn

YOU AIN'T GOTTA SPEAK TO ME

Spiritual Lyrics

How are you doing today?

Silence.

Maybe they just didn't hear.

Maybe I'm just too far away.

I need to get near.

I repeat myself.

Still no answer.

I ask myself if I'm even in this hemisphere.

There's no question nor doubt

about me bein' here.

I'm a soft-spoken person.

Maybe I need to turn it up a notch

and speak a little louder.

If people spoke to me a little more often,

I'd feel prouder.

Now I've got mixed feelings

about the situation.

I'm all mixed up like clam chowder.

Let this problem "poof" be gone

like Johnson baby powder.

Antonio Finn

I know that I'm not the only individual

this has happened to in some degree.

You walk by someone

while walking your dog,

and you speak.

They don't say a word or make a peep.

If I were you, I wouldn't worry about it.

I'd just say to myself,

"I'm still gonna be the same

just like I am every day.

I'll still get my rest tonight

and still will sleep."

In the morning,

I'm gonna thank the lord

for raisin' up this body

and go down on my knee,

believe you me.

I'm gonna fix my breakfast,

and I'm gonna eat.

I'll still be kind and sweet.

Spiritual Lyrics

I want God to guide my mind and steps,

So my heart will never miss a beat.

If people don't know how to love and treat me,

Lord, thanks for stopping by just to greet me.

People, you can just keep goin' by

without uttering a word.

You ain't gotta speak to me.

Antonio Finn

DON'T MESS WITH THE ELECT

Spiritual Lyrics

I can't believe that today

is the day that the Lord hath made

even though it's kinda gray and hazy outside.

I wouldn't in a million years trade.

He has kept me safe.

What a sight.

I pray to God it doesn't fade away.

I'm still well and very much alive.

Some weren't so blessed, but I still strive.

Never letting my guards down, just no jive.

I'll keep all of my trust in Him,

He'll never deprive,

especially if you're His elect,

and it doesn't matter if

I've encountered much reject.

I promise you this,

They can call me everything but a child of God.

They still must show me much respect.

If they won't acknowledge Him,

They'll get a whipping,

Antonio Finn

the worst one of their lives

and one that they'll never forget.

Oh my, when God gets a hold of 'em,

someone needs to be doing much prayin',

'cause they'll deserve every bit of it.

You can't run away from it,

so there won't be any strayin'.

Once God's wrath comes down across,

so-and-so's back stripes gonna be layin'.

They'll be runnin' like they're in a relay race.

You should be a disgrace to the human race.

Why did you try to run?

Come on, man.

With God there isn't going to be any kind of foot chase.

You'd be better off taking your medicine face-to-face.

I bet next time you'll respect one of God's elect

'cause His own people he'll always protect.

Spiritual Lyrics

OH, WHAT A FEELIN'

Antonio Finn

I can't explain the way you make me feel.

It's like my back is up against cold steel.

I asked myself,

can it be all this real?

You hooked me like a fisherman hooks a fish

using a rod and reel.

When I look back over my life,

Nothin' was quite like this,

not even the bottle top that I often gave a twist.

The stuff I smoked had me in a daze, a mist.

After a while it wore off.

Just look at me takin' all those risks.

Hey, I'm sick of this.

I didn't do nothin' but add confusion

to all of the many problems I had.

It wasn't creating any solutions.

I thought that I really was something

when I had a lot in my pocket.

A woman, a car, etc. was all an illusion.

One day I decided to finally meet you.

Spiritual Lyrics

Nothin' else ever satisfied me

or even came close to you.

Oh what a feelin'

just to have somebody listenin'

concerning my blues.

Remember that time I came unglued?

People were spreadin' my business

in the street singin' your news.

Uh huh, it was somebody who was

close tight with you.

Man, I couldn't even see the signs and clues.

I never felt these feelings before.

It's higher than any high with God.

How can one not soar?

If you truly hook up with Him,

everything that oppress you

He'll settle the score.

I can get in the zone

and stay a million miles away.

I love to get in His presence

Antonio Finn

to meditate and pray.

Can you feel and see the illumination all over me?

Can you see the sun's rays all day?

There's a smile on my face.

I'll be grillin',

take a dose of Him, and be just chillin'.

Nothin' else amounts up to God.

Oh, what a feelin'.

Spiritual Lyrics

TAME MY TONGUE

Antonio Finn

I already know.

You don't have to tell me.

It's a cryin' shame.

It's not nobody's fault but mine,

so who's to blame?

I don't believe anyone on earth can say

their tongue is tamed.

It's so full of lies and many games.

It's small but all so powerful.

It has penetrated some of the best of them

and is always talkin'.

It's never full.

Sharp as a razor blade,

It's hardly even dull.

If it's used in an untimely manner,

the tongue can be so sinful.

Eatin' up people right down to the hull.

When anger is involved,

I say things I shouldn't say.

Please don't take it personal,

Spiritual Lyrics

'cause I really don't mean it.

Pray for me concerning this fat loud mouth.

I need a lean kit.

God don't like it when I act ugly toward people

I should know better.

There are many examples,

'cause I've seen it.

Lord, I'll be all right if you'd just tame my tongue.

Spank or whip me not when I'm right

but when I'm wrong,

so I can be a better man.

I apologize,

so I can sing a new song.

I'd like to say so long

you vicious, violent tongue.

When a commandment is made to me that reeks,

I want to shoot off my mouth

like a missile which seeks.

Man, it takes everything in me to continue.

Close up my cheeks

Antonio Finn

I can't take it anymore.

My mouth don't want to hear nothing.

It just wants to take aim.

If I give in,

how could I bear the shame?

Why does this always happen to me?

Can it even ever be contained?

Can anyone answer me or explain?

Maybe I'm just takin' this

situation to the extreme.

Sometimes things aren't always what they seem.

I'm hoping it's all just a bad dream.

I had to blow off some steam.

Spiritual Lyrics

WHEN THE ENEMY STRIKES

Antonio Finn

I'm hit again this morning.

I got struck.

Lord, why me?

Is it a case of bad luck?

Did I miss getting hit hard by a truck?

I must continually call on Jesus' name

to pick me up out of the nasty muck.

If you-know-who had the chance,

he'd kick you back in the dirt.

Ah, shucks.

if he had his way,

the life that's in me,

he'd try to suck.

God keeps me safe in His arms,

'cause He warns His angels in charge of me.

They'll sound the alarms.

Charge is the next thing they'll do.

God said He'd take care of me and you.

He doesn't ever slack in anything.

He doesn't have one or two angels

Spiritual Lyrics

watchin' over us.

He has quite a few.

Listen here.

He provided the word of God.

That's our mighty weapon for the devil,

so go ahead and shoot.

Make sure every morning put on your suit,

and help somebody along the way

who may be weak.

There's strength in numbers,

so there's room to recruit.

Knock down the enemies' camp.

Give 'em the old boot.

In the air they'll go.

They're goin' down fast without a parachute.

Ain't the Lord all right?

Remember you're never alone,

so you must stay in the light.

I don't care if it takes all the strength that's in you.

Sometimes you gotta pray to God

Antonio Finn

with all your heart and might.

Sometimes early in the morning,

all day and all night.

Till you get you-know-who

completely out of your sight.

Tell that fool to take a never-ending flight.

Tell him to take a hike.

Spiritual Lyrics

YOUR NEVER-ENDING LETTER

Antonio Finn

Dear God,

Thanks for Your never-ending letter.

Every time that I read it,

it gets better and better.

How else could I maneuver

through life's bad weather?

How can I hear from You

when I'm feeling weary?

Your letter causes my eyes to be wet.

There goes the tear.

See, Lord?

You always know the right words to say.

You continue to steer me.

I can read Your never-ending letter

any time of the day or night.

It helps me in any situation,

even if I had a fight.

Your letter tells me what to do

to make things all right.

It seems like it will never end.

Spiritual Lyrics

It'll always be here.

It's a blessing to know

it'll be left here with my children.

Jesus thought of me.

He's a true friend.

There are so many of those pages.

It's been around a long time.

Your letter has survived the ages.

I pray the brothers and sisters

will read this letter,

especially the ones who are locked up in cages.

We're all on different levels and stages.

Your never-ending letter is like a run-on sentence.

It keeps goin' on and on.

It's always on time with perfect attendance.

At times I feel lonely.

Then I read your letter.

Now I can feel your wonderful presence.

Out of nowhere, I start to apologize.

Oh boy, I tell you that repentance.

Antonio Finn

Lord, thank you for your never-ending letter

to help me get through life's stormy weather.

Some people don't know which way

the storm is blowin' by using a feather.

Now they're goin' the wrong way.

Don't you know, your body the devil wants to sever?

My soul, devil, you won't get ever.

I'm gonna read Your letter.

I'm here to stay for eternity forever.

Spiritual Lyrics

WHY BRAG?

Antonio Finn

Everybody probably has done this.

It's brag.

Whether it's about cars, a job, a man,

or a small amount of dollars

exaggeratin' is like a bank bag.

You have your new outfit on,

lookin' like you really made it.

Your new shoes and hat have a tag.

Why bother, why brag?

People try hard to do this.

They must not have read the Bible.

Chapter and verse they must have missed.

They don't even know the risk.

Am I that important to you

that you always have to brag

to make yourself look big?

Those are the games people play

when their mentality is that of a kid.

I'm better than that.

I'm gonna stay humble while you look stupid.

Spiritual Lyrics

You really want to wear it?

If I wanted to brag about somebody

it would be God and all of the things He did.

He's the bigwig.

I hope you learned from this.

It's silly,

so why brag about things you could've had?

Hearin' it over and over is quite a drag.

Like a broken record repeatin' itself,

It sounds very sad.

It's not cool spendin' all of your money

to keep up with the latest fads.

You have all that pride.

It only delays your blessing, so why brag?

Things could be a lot better for you,

so why make it bad?

When you read this, if you even do,

I hope you don't get mad.

I can see ya now with your new outfit on,

those pants that sag and those new shoes.

Antonio Finn

Don't forget the new hat with the tag.

If you would read this,

I'd be glad.

Remember this

if nothing else.

Why brag?

Spiritual Lyrics

WHAT NOT TO CHANGE

Antonio Finn

I'm just goin' over a couple of things,

checkin' my list on what not to change

that I really need in my life.

Some people may think it's strange.

I don't want to get out of God's sight or range.

I'll make sure I thank Him for sparin' me

in these last evil days,

'cause this body, He didn't have to raise.

I can see and hear and feel

the sunlight on my face.

With its fiery blaze, I'm gonna make sure

with a loud voice that I'll give him praise.

I won't change the way

I read the Word for at least thirty minutes.

Its nourishing power adds life onto my sentence.

It improves my body for the battle

with much nutrients.

I don't want to change the fact that

if someone does something wrong to me,

to Him belongs the vengeance.

Spiritual Lyrics

I know that sometimes You're displeased.

I have to get down on my knees

and ask for Your forgiveness.

It's hard sometimes to forgive

my troublesome enemies.

After doin' the proper duty,

my mind is at ease.

What not to change.

I must stay God-like,

and remain the same.

I want to keep my composure and remain

in this rollercoaster of a ride game.

What not to change.

Lord, how can we spend quality time together

without the Word every day?

How could one bear

the humiliation and shame?

How could I be alive without You providin'

the blood which runs through my veins

to the heart, back to the brain?

Antonio Finn

With You is where I'll be.

It's where I'm gonna remain.

Spiritual Lyrics

WHO AM I?

Antonio Finn

I'm a person who lifts up a prayer

in the night,

to my Lord, the giving life.

I'm a soldier who's on the battlefield,

eager to war or fight.

I am an honest sinner,

tryin' to make things right.

I am one born of a woman,

a god-like being called a human.

I'm that one who will help a troubled body,

for I'm a good Samaritan.

Most of all, I'm a godly man.

I'm the seed of Eve and Adam,

and also the son of Abraham.

I'm a son of my earthly mother,

cousin, uncle, and also a brother.

I'm a great-grandson to my grandmother's mother.

I'm one who wouldn't want another.

I'm a father and Lord-willing I'll speak it in existence

that I'm a mighty author.

Spiritual Lyrics

I'm one who tries to avoid trouble,

so why bother?

I'm a husband to one woman, my lovely wife,

and a saint that has a brand-new life.

I'm a son of God who rescues me

out of trials and strife.

I'm some lucky aunt's nephew.

I'm the missing in my family

who's concerned about our relationship

on what to do.

If I only knew.

So I turn to God.

I'm a smart student to the Lord

who's a dear friend.

I'm a ghost to the ones

who put on and pretend.

I'm a patient to the doctor Jesus

with my many wounds He'll mend.

I'm His servant.

This is what I strongly intend.

Antonio Finn

I know I'm not a stranger to Him,

and to those who are getting to know Him.

This I strongly recommend.

Who am I?

I'm that child of the Most High

and a very nice guy.

One who daily tries to die.

I'm the son of the Great I Am.

That is who I am.

Spiritual Lyrics

WHY THE ATTITUDE?

Antonio Finn

I woke up this morning feelin' restless

in a bad mood.

Don't ask me why,

'cause I don't know.

This morning I could've given a better answer

instead of being rude.

I'm usually a nice person,

yeah, a fair dude.

So why the attitude?

It's not something I get pleasure out of

or that I enjoy doin'.

I've been battlin' this since I was a little boy.

If I act like this toward you, just overlook me,

'cause I can annoy.

Hey, at least I'm not tryin' to cover it up.

I admit it when I'm wrong.

If I could just stop my attitude

before a leak is sprung.

It's almost like hearin' water drippin'

from the leaky pipes,

Spiritual Lyrics

or a broken record

playin' the same old sad song.

Who wants to hear it or clean up the mess

which was made with a dry sponge

and have to ring it out into a body of water

where it belongs?

I don't care where it ends up,

away from me, gone.

I'd feel much better then.

It's somethin' that I'm goin' to have to

work on every day.

I'm gonna eventually win.

Along the way, Lord, I may ask

that You lend me Your hand.

I don't need to worry about when

You're goin' to free me from this evil sin.

How long will it take before you step in,

my good friend?

If I feel this ugly attitude comin' up,

you have an option.

Antonio Finn

"Pray about it, and give it to Me," says the Lord.

He also says, "That thing in your hand,

you need to drop, son.

This sin needs to go.

it's in the top ten of sins. my child."

It's the top one which really needs to go, Lord.

I'll be glad if You'd get rid of it.

I'll start my day out with caution

and keep from wakin' up in a bad mood

with my face lookin' all ugly and bein' crude.

snappin' at folks bein' silly.

Hey, that's really rude.

I ask myself this question.

Hey, why the attitude?

Spiritual Lyrics

WORDS OF ENCOURAGEMENT

Antonio Finn

Brothers and sisters, I greet you

in the name of Jesus Christ.

You probably won't hear this much,

but God is happy that you've changed your life.

All of the wrong things,

you made up for it,

'cause you finally did something right.

Blessed be you for walking

by faith and not by sight.

These words are for you,

and these are words of encouragement.

You've been doin' so well.

Oh yes, congratulations on

your wedding unto God.

Skip past the engagement.

I pray to God that no one

tells you any words of discouragement,

'cause you may be a little different.

You're God's now.

You're full of gifts.

Spiritual Lyrics

Yes, you're gifted!

You just don't get beside yourself.

Out of your mouth God's name should be lifted.

You should hold on to God

with all of your might.

Tossed and bein' sifted.

You have such a good heart

and when you needed ya help,

you'd never hesitate.

Always in the center of projects,

you don't mind if I ask to participate.

If you're havin' some trouble,

you still make an effort

even though you're runnin' late.

God's love is what you demonstrate.

Many times You've been used

by people close to you.

Never losin' your temper,

you kept your cool.

Standing on the Word and trustin' in God's words

Antonio Finn

never bendin' the rules.

You watched and watched for God to show up.

You stayed awake cryin' your eyes out

on your knees until they started to ache.

Will God ever come through with my big break?

I know you're tired of watchin' out for these snakes.

You did it,

'cause you hung on in there and escaped.

I hope you like these words.

I got to get them to you.

It's urgent.

Just keep followin' Christ and be a faithful servant.

Straight from me to you,

God's word is sent.

Few, but mighty, words of encouragement.

Spiritual Lyrics

STOP COMPLAINING (10-30-04)

Antonio Finn

I know we all have done it before

complaining about how something

isn't going our way.

It's just within our core.

The funny thing about that is

it only takes one individual

to open up the door.

Now it's a few more than you had before.

You have to try to ignore.

If it happens in the house of God with words

that are coming from behind me,

it's complaining.

Now I'm doing it again.

I'm complaining and not following

my Father's instruction or training.

The Lord allowed manna to fall from above.

It was a type of bread.

Man, were they filled.

He told them to fill up one bowl

of His daily bread,

Spiritual Lyrics

but some got greedy and exceeded the limit.

Some complained about the bread.

Now they wanted meat

which the almighty God fed.

It was filled with disease which spread.

As a result of complaining

3 and 200 hundred thousand fell dead.

I don't know about you,

but as for me,

I'm gonna try not to complain

about the pain that resulted

from a back sprain.

It's time for me to exit this train.

These words are so very true.

Nothin' under the sun is new.

The words are always explaining

the dangers of complaining,

so please follow the instruction of the

Bible and heed to the Lord's training.

Stop complaining.

Antonio Finn

11-25-04 THANKS FOR GIVIN'

Spiritual Lyrics

Lord, thanks for givin' the life of breath.

Even though sometimes I don't feel so good inside,

You still bless me with great health.

When I need money in a situation.

from out of nowhere You rain down Your wealth.

He's a present help in the time of need

for you and me.

Lord, wherever You are is where a saint ought to be.

Today isn't the only day I want to thank Thee

for each and every day I see.

I thank You, Lord, 'cause at one time

I was in bondage,

but now I'm set free.

Just take a look around at what

He's done for you and me.

Our sins are piling way up,

but they aren't forgotten at this moment.

They're bein' cast into the sea, Lord.

I thank you for planting Your word and the seed.

at that time in my life. Lord,

Antonio Finn

You saw how glad I was You showed up

and blessed me according to my needs.

What would I do without the bread

You feed both carnal and spiritually?

Sometimes I get beside myself

then out comes Your rod or reed.

Thank you for the whippin'

even though I don't really like it.

No matter how I try to plead, Lord,

You know just what I need,

'cause You love me.

God, thanks for givin' up Your Son for our sake,

which is a present help, indeed,

especially if you're sufferin' from a lack of needs.

He'll answer yes or no, fast and slow.

Child, just learn how to wait on Him.

He may answer at high speed.

It's all based according to your need.

Lord thanks for givin' me this brand-new life.

I even thank you for my tribulations, struggles and strife.

Spiritual Lyrics

I thank you for my son and my tender-hearted wife.

Thanks for all of my sisters and brothers.

Thanks for still havin' old grandma,

and I can't forget my wonderful mother,

aunts, uncles, and cousins.

Lord, let the little love that we have never end.

We used to be knitted tight.

I don't know what happened to us.

Lord, I know that one day

you'll tighten back up the covers.

Lord, save 'em.

I'll make sure, Lord, to give You thanks

for everything you do.

I'll not just goin' to thank you for one day

but for every day that I see.

We could find something to thank God for every day.

if you can't find anything

what about the sacrifice of His Son?

Thanks for givin'.

Antonio Finn

1-3-05 SPIRITUAL LYRICS

Spiritual Lyrics

This will only take a few minutes of your time,

and thanks for invitin' me.

Sometimes the way I talk can be quite frightenin',

but I don't mean any harm.

The words God gave me

are spoken to enlighten you,

'cause some people's eyes are still closed.

After I'm done with you,

I bet ya they'll soon widen.

Your range of vision is far ahead,

and you'll be very visual.

These words aren't just any words that are spoken.

They're lyrics that are spiritual,

I pray the Holy Ghost shows up really soon.

I can't wait.

Do you want to know why?

He loves to get physical.

It's all good though,

'cause pretty soon you're gonna receive a miracle.

Believe you me,

Antonio Finn

I know we all have many problems.

I know how ya feel ranging from stressin' about finances,

to car payments or wonderin' where

the next meal is comin' from.

It wouldn't hurt if people treated you better.

Unfortunately, you got a raw deal.

I got somethin' for that, though.

The words which I speak are so real.

If you don't believe me,

just read the book God blessed

me to write and soon reveal.

I promise it'll open your eyes

like the juice that squirts in your eyes

from an orange.

It'll mend and bind up your wounds,

so you can finally heal,

and this goes farther than physics.

I don't think there's nothin' else

out there like my words.

Nothin' else mimics them.

Spiritual Lyrics

The Lord's healin' words,

which He allowed me to borrow,

are also spiritual lyrics.

These words God gave me will help your range,

so you can see far ahead.

You'll be very visual.

These aren't just any words that are spoken.

They're lyrics that are spiritual.

I pray the Holy Ghost shows up really soon.

I can't wait.

Do you want to know why?

He likes to get physical.

It's all good though,

'cause pretty soon you're gonna receive a miracle.

I give ya spiritual lyrics.

Antonio Finn

SOME SAY IT'S NOT A GOOD DAY (11-9-04)

Spiritual Lyrics

I can hear 'em mumblin' and complain'

cause outside it looks kinda hazy,

but to me it's a blessed day.

You always seem to amaze me.

I've still got a smile on my face.

People look at me like I'm crazy.

Even though it's goin' to rain,

if you're alive and well today,

Thank Him.

Oh yes, even for your pain.

Some weren't so blessed.

They can't say the same.

Thank God you're not in a pine box

covered in wood grain.

Somebody's family is sufferin' with many ails.

Their loved one gave up the ghost,

and left their shell.

You ought to be thankin' God.

I don't know about you,

but I'm gonna yell I'm blessed to be alive.

Antonio Finn

Can't you tell?

Just look around at His blessings, my brother and sister.

Time to take off the veil.

Look down at your feet.

Some don't have nothin'.

Look in the fridge.

You got plenty to eat

when some are wishin' they

had a barrel of wheat.

He offered us a deal of a lifetime

that the devil can't ever beat.

What a treat.

This is a day I didn't regret.

My God thought about me.

The table has already been set.

You know it only drizzled a little bit,

and it didn't really get wet.

I thank Him for bein' eyes for me

and keepin me from gettin trapped

in the enemy's net.

Spiritual Lyrics

He takes care of His elect.

Lord, You get much respect.

I don't want to hear the bad news blues station

another someone needs to select.

Anyway, some say it's not a good day.

In reality, if you're alive and well today,

It's a God blessed day

Antonio Finn

1-4-05   SOMETHIN' NEEDS TO GIVE

Spiritual Lyrics

Oh, here I go again on my way

Up another steep hill.

Lord, You made it loud and clear

that I'm supposed to trust in You

and just be still.

That's not the way I feel.

Sometimes I'm pressed so much

like my back is up against the millstone.

I'm goin' through a mill of trials.

That's why I'm tryin' to get it together.

I don't know why it always seems

like I'm always wantin' to do things on my own.

It never works out.

Lord, when are You comin'?

I'm in desperate need.

Can You please give me somethin'?

I'll be looking out for Your blessings

to just start pumpin'

out of the sky like an automatic

double-barreled shotgun.

Antonio Finn

Lord, You can see that I'm kinda worn out and tired.

My tongue is cleavin' to the roof of my mouth.

I'm overheated with the devil,

and I can't wait till he's cooked and well done.

You're the one I admire,

and as You can tell,

I'm very fond of You.

I definitely like the way You handle things,

and the victory here is already won.

Never again will my enemies be able to see me

Sufferin' in my adversities.

Hopefully, there'll be no more misery,

'cause this isn't how I want to live anymore.

I understand that sometimes

I have to climb up hills.

Lord, one thing You made loud and clear.

I'm supposed to just be still,

but that isn't the way I feel.

Sometimes I'm pressed so much

like my back is against the millstone.

Spiritual Lyrics

I'm goin' through a mill of trials.

That's why I'm tryin to get it together.

I don't know why it always seems

like the enemy wants to destroy me.

He wants to kill us all,

and he thrives off fear.

He gets a thrill off of us gettin' scared.

Lord, You won't let him

have his way with me, though.

Please, Lord, somethin' needs to give.

Antonio Finn

1-10-05 LORD, SHOW UP, SHOW OUT

Spiritual Lyrics

I'm sittin' here with my big bag of troubles,

and I know right now, Lord, You can show up.

It's gettin' too heavy for me

to carry it all by myself.

I'm sinkin' down in the muck.

I can't see the trouble which lies ahead of me.

Can you tell me when to duck?

Don't forget to knock it out of here

like those hockey players strike a puck.

Yeah, Lord, knock it to Thy kingdom.

I'm gonna be lookin' soon to come.

I understand it's not gonna be based on my will.

Lord, Your will be done.

Lord, whenever You decide to come,

show out 'cause right now I'm needy.

Ya know, I'm livin' in the land of drought.

The ones who seen me cryin' once before

won't ever see me pout.

Lord, You don't do small things,

but Ya love to do big things,

Antonio Finn

and those are wise words

that are spoken from my heart

out through my mouth.

So, Lord, if You want to just show out,

I'll forget what people say,

and I'll follow only Your guidance.

I'm gonna continue to trust You'll do something big,

so I'll keep my reliance in You, Lord.

Things are lookin' kind of slim right now,

so it wouldn't hurt it if You'd bless my finances.

I'll make sure that everything I do

will be in compliance with You.

Lord, please show up.

I'm meant to be eatin' steaks, no cold cuts.

Instead of bein' down,

I'm about to blow up.

I'm gonna be somebody special.

Lord, Ya need to really

turn some heads and show out.

My cup is so overflowing

Spiritual Lyrics

that it flows out.

If you ask if God will come through,

I'll tell ya there's no doubt.

Hey, listen.

I'm sittin' here with my big bag of troubles.

I know right now, Lord, that You show up.

It's getting' too heavy

for me to carry it all by myself.

I'm sinkin' down in the muck.

I can't see the troubles which lies ahead.

Can Ya tell me when to duck?

Lord, please show up and show out.

Antonio Finn

12-14-04   SIMPLY SORROW

Spiritual Lyrics

Why do you sob,

and for what reason are you cryin'?

I bet life's struggles have got you down,

and if there were such a ticket,

I'd be buyin' my way out of trouble.

If I were you,

I hope all of my troubles would be expirin'.

It's all simply sorrow.

If I can just make it through,

there's hope for me tomorrow.

It's only for a little while

that the tree looks dry, rotten, and hollow.

If you mock the steps that lead to life,

you need to make sure

it's the Lord's steps you follow.

I know why sometimes it's us who often weep,

'cause a friend or our loved one has fallen asleep.

God understands all of our pain.

That's why, when one is laid to rest,

the rain seeps down in the earth so deep,

Antonio Finn

it's reminding us that,

if they were saved,

their soul He'll keep.

A woman goes through the pain and sorrow

to bear a child.

It's only for a short period of time,

for only in a little while

she collects herself

and sees that she and the baby

made it through all of the turmoil.

She smiles.

That's very good news for her,

since it's all over the things

that were all so scary.

Like it was for her,

it also applies to us all.

It reminds us that our sorrows

are just temporary.

We all need to remember

that good and evil are always battling each other,

Spiritual Lyrics

and they're both to one another quite contrary.

Don't you fret.

The Lord brought us this far.

He'll still carry us over to the other side.

Saints, over there we'll forever tarry.

I understand clearly

that our sorrows are not simply

what we prefer to go through,

They'll make us both feel lost and empty.

Who's to say anything about it,

cause God decides what's best for us,

and He determines our destiny.

I guess our sorrow works out

for our good, evidently.

I'll hold onto my faith in God

a little longer.

I may need to borrow some faith

that'll tide me over,

so I can see how God will bless me tomorrow.

Hopefully something good will come

Antonio Finn

out of all of my troubles.

It's simply sorrow.

Spiritual Lyrics

12-5-04   SAY THE WORD

Antonio Finn

My mouth will be lifted up on high,

as long as I say the Word.

First thing in the morning I'm gonna

strap up and gird up my body,

'cause the enemy will send someone

or something to keep You from bein' heard.

There's a chapter in the Bible that could help you.

It's in the 25th chapter of Proverbs.

You need to believe in yourself

that what you say will come to pass.

There can't be any doubt.

You want to be blessed richly

and not be in the land of drought.

You shouldn't blame anyone at all.

You might as well blame your mouth.

You should want your words to speak life only

and not your own damnation.

If you just happen to mess up after bein' told,

I want to hear your explanation.

Did you bump your head,

Spiritual Lyrics

or do you need your head checked out

by havin' a psychological evaluation?

I'm serious.

This decision may affect you, possibly for the duration.

Just say the word to all of your problems,

'cause I know personally firsthand

they can be stressful and very bothersome.

They won't stand a chance up against the Word.

They're finished, and they're done.

Sayin the Word can move your mountains,

even if you have more than one problem.

There's enough holy water that could bless you.

It's in the Lord's fountain.

Count your many blessings.

You don't even have to be an accountant.

Use your fingers and toes.

It doesn't really matter.

Just make sure you count em'.

If you allow bad words to utter out,

as a result of your doubt,

Antonio Finn

you need to bind them up quickly,

so they fall to the ground and die, not sprout up.

Saints, don't allow bad words to come out of your mouth.

Only say the Word

to get your blessing in Jesus' name.

It's all yours and all you gotta do is make a claim.

Watch the blessing and just watch out,

'cause God will make it rain.

I'll sing out with a loud cry,

so I can be heard

saying a few adjectives, nouns, and maybe a verb.

Today I'll just say the Word.

Spiritual Lyrics

SATAN GET BEHIND ME

Antonio Finn

He comes often when I'm reading God's

holy Word on my bed.

Why bother me?

Just look right over there.

Do you see Joe and Marvin?

Why not bother them instead?

You see, devil, my Lord already beat

you a long time ago.

Don't you remember what happened on Calvary?

I'm so sick and tired of you trying to distort my mind.

"Satan, get behind me."

That's right, you stinkin' blue-headed fool!

I'm tired of fantasizing about chicks

I could've or should've split.

I imagine them in the bed with me havin' sex,

until finally my heart gets touched by the Holy Spirit.

That ol' Satan even attacks me

when I'm on my way to the house of worship.

My main purpose for being there is to hear God's word.

Instead I look under skirts for a peek and those spirits,

Spiritual Lyrics

which I'm entertaining at that time,

paints a wicked picture of them in t-backs or bikinis.

That's not godly!

I've already committed a sin,

because I'm lusting after them.

"Satan, get behind me!"

Why are you still messin' with me?

Of all people, just look right over there.

Do you see Gary, Rick or Boboh?

It almost slipped my mind.

Ol' slew has been around awhile,

and he's just doin' his job.

He spends his days walkin' about

lurking to and fro seeking whom

he may devour, kill, steal, and destroy.

We're forgettin' about one thing.

He likes making a lot of noise,

because he doesn't have any teeth

that can bite us saints,

so he's just a play toy.

Antonio Finn

Many people have a false impression

that he's red all over with a pitchfork in hand.

He may be in the form of a man, woman, or even a baby.

He also can transform himself into an angel of light.

"Satan, get behind me."

Remember that the devil is very clever

and a compulsive liar.

Never believe anything he says.

He's also a thief.

Ol' slew foot has deceived many

and stole from kids, disciples, Pharisees,

kings and even from the highest of chiefs.

Don't ya dare think that the ol' sorry ol' punk

will fight you head-up,

'cause he won't.

Instead, he catches you off guard with a sucker punch.

This is just a hunch.

Believe me, he'll use whomever allows him to use them.

It may be a sister, brother, wife, kids

even your own dear mother.

Spiritual Lyrics

He doesn't care.

Listen to this.

I don't want just some of my things.

I want them all.

Hey, devil, give me my wife, my kids, and freedom.

Don't give him any kind of slack.

Hey, devil, you've used me long enough.

I belong to the most-high God,

and He owns everything that you took.

He's giving it all back!

Since you couldn't listen, devil,

you're headed for life without parole in hell.

Hey, devil, looks like you lose.

My Lord has all the keys to

everything you thought ya had.

Sorry, you have to be condemned to hell for eternity.

Sorry, those are just God's rules.

Thank you, Lord, for dying on the cross

to save us all who believe.

You saved me, my brother, and all of my family.

Antonio Finn

Lord, ya didn't have to, but you did.

Thank you for giving up your life

on the ol' rugged cross,

and thanks for giving us another chance.

"Satan get behind me!"

Spiritual Lyrics

PUT THE WORDS IN MY MOUTH (10-21-04)

Antonio Finn

I want you to put the words in my mouth.

Make the right ones come out,

because I don't think before I shout.

Give my brain something to think about.

Put the words in my mouth,

so I don't get writa's block.

Give me those filling words,

so I can feed the flocks,

'cause time's running out.

No need to watch the clocks.

Some are so thirsty they need

the living water on the rocks.

If I had your words in my mouth

I wouldn't have messed up today.

I shouldn't have said those devilish words.

Guess I had to have it my way.

Your words say if we could speak a kind word

when speak to people

I wouldn't speak so rough.

I guess it's a way of life for me

Spiritual Lyrics

'cause I was brought up tough.

It all started that day when my boys said,

"Come on, take a puff."

Since then it's been fightin', shootin', killin'

A long journey of wild livin'.

Lord, I've had enough.

Put the words in my mouth

for the ones who say I ain't wrapped too tight.

I'm speaking these words.

Everything will be all right.

Keep your head up,

cause in this day and age

we must continue the fight.

Antonio Finn

PRESS, OUT COMES THE BEST

Spiritual Lyrics

Will it ever end?

You know I'm getting' sick of this.

All of these problems are weighing me down.

Erase some of them off my list,

I don't want my health to be at risk

or be mad at You, Father.

Yellin' hands in the air and shakin' my fist.

Could it all be happening for a reason?

People are always lyin' to and about me

addin' their season,

then come back in my face sayin', "I'm just teasin'."

Lord, what is the purpose?

If I wanted to get picked on

or make people laugh,

I'd have joined the circus.

My problems sometimes are many.

These words don't even scratch the surface.

Lord, is all my life worthwhile,

or is it worthless?

It's like someone pushed a button on me that says,

Antonio Finn

"Press, out comes the best."

How many are there?

I'm, talkin' about the tests.

Don't forget that I need your help.

Rescue me right away via-express now.

I kinda understand that

after I get squeezed,

I'll humble myself and call on You

to lend me a helpin' hand.

When a lemon is pressed it's not so good,

but add sugar then you get lemonade.

After the war,

I'll lick my wounds and ask Father to heal me.

I don't need a Band-Aid.

Glad you showed when you did.

I'm still here.

I didn't fade away.

Sit back and talk to you, relaxing in the shade.

I can finally get a bit of rest

even though they were many.

Spiritual Lyrics

With your help, I passed the tests.

It wasn't easy, though

perhaps kinda restless.

Go through it, you won't regret.

It's for your good.

God bless.

You'll see that it'll benefit you,

and you get pressed, out comes the best.

Antonio Finn

1-11-05 PLANT DA SEED

Spiritual Lyrics

I'm done with packin' up all of my bags,

'cause I'm gonna go on a little trip, an adventure.

It's time to get the word out.

The Lord said, "My son, it's time for you

to minister to the people who are lost."

I'll do what Ya say, Lord, You're my mentor.

If I could, I'd plant it all over the world

just like that guy who walked barefooted

with his hat, pants, and suspenders.

He spent his entire life walkin' the earth,

plantin' a very small object

which eventually developed into a tree.

Most of you may know

or may have heard of him before.

I'll give you a hint.

His first name is Johnny.

Just as he did,

I also want to go around and plant da seed.

Do you want to know the best thing about it?

My man done it from his heart freely.

Antonio Finn

Even though my wicked flesh

may get weak sometimes,

and I might say what's the use

'cause they may not want to accept or hear me

then I'll want to give 'em the boot.

I can't be like that though,

'cause I now work for the Lord,

and I gotta be patient, not a brute.

Why do I still walk by sight and not by faith?

Who knows if the seed hasn't already taken root?

The tree isn't always dead

just because we don't see any fruit.

God does.

Without Him, we wouldn't even have a chance

to be able to go out and plant

the lost souls.

We were poor ol' peasants and Gentiles,

but He still took us in.

Lord, thanks for the salvation present,

and please protect us from the wicked ones

Spiritual Lyrics

who may hate our harsh words.

Some of them might not be

pleasant to a sinner's ear,

so I guess I'll be on my way.

I'm done with packin' up all of my bags.

I'm goin' on a little trip, an adventure.

I'm doin' a good deed.

The people are very much in desperate need.

Lord, my hands are full,

and there are many mouths to feed.

Just like that guy, I also want to plant da seed.

Antonio Finn

1-12-05 POETIC ELIXIR

Spiritual Lyrics

As you can tell by now

I have a way with words.

Please excuse me 'cause I forgot to warn you.

All of my words don't go down so smooth.

Some people just can't stand it

when I speak the Word 'cause

it ain't nothin' but da truth.

It can be just like vinegar

that may be aggravatin' a sinner's tooth,

and it's not all that bad.

If people obey 'em

they can heal, and they can also soothe.

Ya wanna know the good thing about it?

You can get it anytime.

Who needs an appointment?

All you have to do is just read the Bible

and get jointed up with the Lord.

He'll save your soul,

and there'll be no more heartaches or disappointments.

Lord, You satisfy your anointed saints.

Antonio Finn

Please give us a double portion of your ointment

which allows me to use words which rhyme that poetic elixir.

I don't even know what comes over me sometimes.

It's You, Lord, who triggers me off.

I don't know how I come up

with these awesome poems,

but their words are from You, God.

They're a perfect mixture of

Your healin' words and prayers

which will paint the perfect picture

for everyone, including the pope.

Life for us can be so hard sometimes,

but I know we could use something or

some encouraging words

to help us cope with the problems of life.

I need for you to please pay very close attention

to what I'm about to say

and think on the things which I speak about.

It's just like lookin' through a scope.

We'll see life more clearly

Spiritual Lyrics

than we've seen it before.

We'll have a better end

'cause we'll have hope.

I don't know about you,

but as for me,

I'm not tryin' to burn or boil in the lake of fire

which I've heard is seven times hotter than our earthly fire

or our oven coils.

I've already been through many heartaches, pains, and toils,

so why would I want to go through all of that?

That's why I must unto God stay loyal.

Me and you, my friend, have to get it right eventually

and keep it straight before we're buried deep down in the soil.

If we don't get it right with God,

we'll be thrown away like a piece of foil.

Then it would be too late,

but thank God we're saved.

I don't know what comes over me sometimes.

I know it's something you do that triggers me off.

I don't know how I come up

Antonio Finn

with these awesome poems,

but I know they're words from God

which are a perfect mixture of

Your healin' words and power

which will paint the perfect picture

that life for us all won't always be like this.

It will get better in the end.

So, Lord, please give me a double portion of Your anointing

Yes, an extra kicker

of words which rhyme with poetic elixir.

Spiritual Lyrics

12-17-04 OVERWORKED UNDERPAID

Antonio Finn

I'm working my butt off

and for what?

I'm overworked and underpaid.

I put up with the boss' attitude.

You see how the boss behaves toward me,

and it's like I'm working for nothin'

as if I were a Hebrew slave.

How can I possibly make it?

How can I provide for my family's sake

while someone else is livin' lovely?

I'm livin' paycheck to paycheck.

I'm workin' so hard

I'm just about to fall out.

Let's not even talk about the pain

in my lower back and neck.

Pretty please, sir,

can I take an early break?

I'll only be a sec.

"No you can't, man."

A dog gets treated with more respect than I do.

Spiritual Lyrics

God of grace, I know You see how

I work my fingers to the bone.

If You just get me through this wilderness,

I'll make sure I pray for all of us

who are goin' through.

I'm not alone.

I'm watchin' the clock.

For a minute there,

it just looked like it went backward.

Man, I know I wanna go home.

I'm so tired of workin' for this stinking devil.

I know that through You, Lord,

one day, You'll give me my own business.

I often read my Bible

and pray on my breaks

so I can remain strong.

If I don't do it,

I'll probably go off or snap on someone.

Why are they taking money out of my pocket?

They love to tap.

Antonio Finn

I'm about to lose it,

so I'll just count from one to ten.

In my once big pile of money

why is there a big gap?

If you ain't making $8.00 and up

you're at a dead-end job.

Yes, it's a trap.

We must hold on to our faith in God.

Let's stay good and tight with Him

like a burrito wrap.

Let's also break all of the curses

of workin' just to make another man rich.

We slave for pennies,

and then if something happens,

you'll have to spend all your money

that you saved for emergencies.

It would be a much-different story

if we'd get a paycheck

for our hard work and abilities.

Unfortunately, we're just paid

Spiritual Lyrics

        the wages of a Hebrew slave.

        We're all definitely overworked underpaid.

Antonio Finn

12-2-04   NOT FOR PROFIT

Spiritual Lyrics

I'm called to be a servant of the Lord

and to serve Him forever.

I don't know why so much is happening

in the world today that's making many people very disturbed.

They can do without more bad news.

Instead, they should be hearin' God's holy word.

It'll give 'em the life they really deserve.

Why are folks more concerned about money

goin in their pocket,

when they should be gettin' saved

'cause hell doesn't have any faucets?

Maybe now they'll think about doin' things

hopefully not for profit.

Come on, people, and help someone

Who's worse off than you and

who's hurting and heartbroken.

They may have told you that

everything just isn't workin' out

no matter how hard they tried.

As they're tellin' you all of this

Antonio Finn

they're cryin' and chokin'.

Hey, a kind lovin' word could save them.

If some help is needed

the Bible has many well-spoken words.

It's not all about makin' a couple dollars.

That isn't what life's all about, my friend.

After we're saved, our obligation

is to lead others to Christ,

especially before the world ends.

There's nothin' wrong with helpin' someone

out with a little money.

Go ahead.

Place it in their hand to show some love to the poor.

When you do this good deed unto God, saint,

fret not 'cause, for your generosity,

He'll return it back to you one hundredfold.

Don't you know that someone may be able

to use your help,

and they may really need to be consoled today?

This should be all our goals.

Spiritual Lyrics

It's more precious than receiving silver and gold.

Do you want know what it is?

It's for us to save as many souls as we can.

These are words which are comin'

from one of God's royal prophets.

Please help someone out

instead of worryin' about

what's goin' to go in your pocket.

Just do it from your heart

not expectin' anything back

and hopefully doin' it not for profit.

Antonio Finn

12-6-04   NO GOVERNMENT SUPPORT

Spiritual Lyrics

They had me running around in circles

like my head was cut off just like a chicken.

They had me goin' back and forth

with all of my problems

which they never really intended on fixin'.

You still end up with a much-bigger bag of mess.

I guess there will be more wounds

for me to be lickin'.

Where is it?

I haven't seen no government support.

Okay, maybe they'll give me

a little bit of food of some sort.

Tell me how I can pay my bills with that,

or how I can hold down the fort.

Some people think they're better than us.

Yeah, right.

Then why do some of them still end up in court?

I'm sayin' they make you almost run a marathon

just for you still not to be helped.

They just don't know how they made me feel.

Antonio Finn

At least, Jesus does.

That's why Jesus wept for us.

If I only knew that this was goin to happen,

I would've just stayed in my bed and slept.

How come when you ask them for help,

they act like it comes out of their pockets?

What they need to do is quit trippin'

and they need to just stop it.

No government support.

They'll slam the door right in your face,

and they expect you to go through

whatever for you to unlock it.

Man, they're about to make me

start poppin' out sprockets.

If you want somethin' from them,

you've got to be aggressive toward 'em

'cause if you don't,

they'll play you, especially if you're too kind.

That's just the government's job.

Their job is to make you quit,

Spiritual Lyrics

and that's just its making.

That's how it's designed.

There's one thing you need to

make note of and keep in mind.

Don't be in a rush.

Just take calculated steps,

and take your time.

The Lord said this,

"If you seek, ye shall find."

They are helpin' the poor get poorer

while the rich just keep on gettin' richer.

I guess they don't really care what happens to us.

Can you see what's wrong with this picture?

My pockets are still gettin' thinner,

while their pockets are steady gettin' bigger and bigger.

That's why I'm not gonna support no government.

Antonio Finn

12-14-04   MY WEAK FLESH

Spiritual Lyrics

Sometimes I feel I can no longer go on,

and I'm feelin' so weak.

This hill isn't getting any shorter,

but it's still very steep.

I haven't heard from the one I daily seek.

I'm not goin' to give up now.

Sometimes, I admit I act a little selfish.

When I see that other people are doin' just fine,

I begin to start acting hellish toward them.

God, why isn't this happening to them?

I'm goin through hell.

I bind you, devil, in the name of Jesus.

That was just my weak flesh talking.

I'm bein' tested by God

to see how well I stand in my faith.

I wonder is it smaller than a mustard seed,

or is it greater?

For me to survive all of these trials,

I'm gonna need more than an eighth.

What I really need to do

Antonio Finn

is get rid of this old flesh,

so I'll go down in the water to bathe.

For me to think of it

is all so thrilling,

and there's a well-known saying the flesh is weak,

but the spirit is always willing.

It wouldn't bother me to know

that the water might send a cold feeling

right up my spine.

I don't care, Lord,

Just get this old flesh out of the way.

I don't know if You'd rip or tear the mess out,

but please be easy with me,

'cause I'm a human being,

and my life renew it.

Lord, go ahead and spare.

I know things happen for a reason,

and sometimes life doesn't seem fair,

but, Lord, I thank You anyway.

I don't want to be like I used to be,

Spiritual Lyrics

and I don't want to go back there.

I wouldn't dare.

Over the years I've made

a big mess out of my life,

but the Lord always knows how

to fix a person up right.

It was me that You dressed up.

You also helped me make it through

all of my many trials and tests.

I didn't even think I'd last another week.

Lord, You knew how much I could stand,

and You knew I was almost about to reach my peak.

I thank You, Lord, for steppin' in

or I wouldn't have made it through this far.

I thank God that I didn't perish.

I'm askin' that You continue

to heal me from this burden, Lord.

Please heal my weak flesh.

Antonio Finn

MY LONG JOURNEY (11-6-04)

I came a long way,

but I still have a long journey.

Some might say, "Yes, you do."

Tell ya stop judging me.

I've been diggin' new wells

every time haters excel.

I kept goin' down those

sometimes dark, lonely trails.

I can't count how many times down I fell.

I says to myself, "Oh, well."

I must keep goin' on my

seemingly never-ending journey.

If I live through it another day,

I can voice my story.

I'm gonna take my time.

What's the hurry?

Even though times are gettin' shorter

and fear sets in,

Spiritual Lyrics

I'm not goin' to worry,

'cause I have faith in my Lord,

and I'm drivin' a Toyota

not a Ford.

I've gotta have it not in reverse but forward.

The crops are ready to be harvested,

so it's time to take in the hoard.

If ya'll are with me,

let's jump aboard.

I'm gonna stay on the J train.

What do I have to lose?

There's a whole lot of gain.

This I know.

If I don't accomplish nothin' else,

eternal life I must obtain.

All my days aren't full of sunshine.

Might get a little bit stormy.

I'm not scared of the rain.

One foot in front of another all up over rocks.

Some of you tried to close

Antonio Finn

the doors and lock the locks.

My God holds the keys.

Whatcha mocks?

Things might be smooth sailing now,

but up ahead holes may be in the road.

Hope you've got shocks.

I must continue, not yet knowin'

where I'm goin'.

Ignore the storm clouds,

'cause I see 'em formin'.

Lord, things look a little bit blurry.

You can see how it'll turn out.

Keep it sturdy,

'cause I mess up sometimes.

You don't judge me like a judge and jury

Spiritual Lyrics

12-7-04 MOTIVATION

Antonio Finn

I'm feelin' kind of lazy today.

Lord, please give me a little extra push,

so I can have enough power

to get around my enemies' ambush.

If they get too close to me,

I'll knock 'em down with the word of God,

'cause they're much too soft

that they're plush toys.

I can't let anything get in my way

that could keep me from reachin' my goals.

I'm tellin' you I've got so much motivation,

and the table is finally turning in my life.

It's in rotation right now as I speak.

You might not see it now,

'cause the Lord is moving me along slowly.

I don't care how slow it's goin'

just as long as the big wheels keep on turning.

This fire which burns toward you

that's in my heart doesn't go out.

It keeps on burning.

Spiritual Lyrics

I want to keep my faith in you, God,

and for me to never give up on anything every day

This is what I'm learning.

Even though doors have gotten closed in my face,

I still pursue my transactions.

I have to stay motivated

and not be so focused on this trouble,

'cause it's only a fraction of things to come.

When things start shakin' up,

my wheels gotta keep their traction gaining.

It's very easy to say it,

but it takes action.

I've got to follow through with it.

I'm so tired of always bein' leveled to the ground.

Sometimes it gets so lonely,

and when you're goin' through it,

no one can be located or found.

It's not goin' to do me any good

to feel like this at this moment, not right now.

That's why I'm gonna get up from here,

Antonio Finn

and I'm not goin' to just sit here

bein' lazy and just lyin' down.

I'm reachin' out for my goals

which are in the skylight,

and there's no limit to what I can achieve,

so I'm gonna go for the highest heights.

My God gave me this power to do my very best

so I know my rights that I have in the Lord.

Lay it all on me, Lord.

You know your powerful motivation,

which I can find in your never-ending

letter or your letter of notification

which can also keep my head above the water.

Yes, it's also a flotation device.

Lord, I appreciate all the things You do for me.

I'm takin' in all donations

from You, Lord,

especially of Your empowering motivation.

Spiritual Lyrics

MOTHER TO THE MOTHERLESS

Antonio Finn

I didn't lose my mother from death

like some people have,

so I can't feel your pain.

We aren't equal,

but most of her life was on needles.

It's not what you think.

She's at the point of bein' impaired,

but it's not her fault,

'cause my father died.

She really misses him and

all of the times they shared.

Mom, you did what you could do,

and I know dearly for us you cared.

A single mother with two kids to raise on your own.

I know you were often scared at times.

I remember I would check on you

to see if you were still awake,

even though I was taking a chance,

'cause it was really late.

I'd ask, "Are you all right?"

Spiritual Lyrics

Then you'd say, "Go back to bed. Mama's okay."

I knew that you weren't.

You probably were tryin' to figure out

how you'd get our next plate.

Oh yeah, Mom, that grin was really fake.

God gave a special love bond

between a mother and a child

even though I got it sometimes,

then you'd have a spell actin' all wild.

Is this the same woman who had so much class

and the one that stayed in style?

I wish I could find the cure to help you, Mom.

If I had to, I'd walk an extra mile.

I remember when my mother was pregnant

with my baby brother.

I'm the baby.

I don't want you, Mom, to have another.

I felt that all of the love was goin'

to my oldest sister and baby brother.

I became very jealous.

Antonio Finn

Nobody cares about me.

Of course, the next thing you know

to Mom and Grandma

I became rebellious.

This is something that all middle kids

become jealous of their siblings.

I should've leaped at the duty toward the situation,

and I should have been zealous.

Mom, your anger toward me was wrong,

but I know you didn't mean it.

Oh, boy when you said "jump"

for me to clean somethin',

I knew that I had to clean it up quick

'cause, Mom, you would steam quick.

You've been through a lot of things.

You've been there, done that, and seen it.

Mom, you're my girl.

Around you my world rotates.

Remember the times we used to

dance around and swirl?

Spiritual Lyrics

When you weren't there,

I had God.

We're like two peas in a pod.

You might have spared me,

but if I get out of line,

He won't, Mom.

I won't listen to people,

when they say, "Your mom left you.

Your sister, your brother, and you lonely."

That can't be true.

It's a bunch of bologna.

I try to separate myself from people

who are so phony.

When you left to get help, God,

and Grandma was there,

and them only.

Mom, now all the times you say

you love me, kiss and hug me,

I ain't gonna lie.

Sometimes, you bug me.

Antonio Finn

Never away from me,

You're still petty with your smile, Mama.

You're still dark and lovely.

You smile now.

You say it loudly

that you're very proud of me.

Okay now, Mom, relax and get some rest.

Those spells were caused by years of stress.

May God heal you, and may He bless.

Nothing more, nothing less.

I've been through much distress,

or just don't have a mother anymore.

He's a mother to the motherless.

Spiritual Lyrics

12-7-04 MIND STAYED ON THEE

Antonio Finn

I got a lot on my mind.

Is it comin', or is it goin'?

I need Your help out of this

blizzard of bad thoughts.

Lord, I mean it's really snowin'.

It's rainin' down cats and dogs in my mind.

I'm tellin' You, Lord, that it's really pourin'.

It's enough to almost drive a person

insane and out of their mind

or even drive 'em looney.

I'll keep this in mind.

That's just part of the process of God's pruning.

I'll be cool about it,

and it wouldn't hurt it

if I had my mind on Your station for a change.

So, Lord, go ahead and adjust me

to do the correct tuning.

Lord, help me keep my mind on Thee.

I know You died upon the cross

a long time ago.

Spiritual Lyrics

Not for me to continue to be in bondage

but for Your manservant to become free.

If I could think of You a lot more

my mind would be in perfect peace.

Thank you, Lord, even though

I'm still havin' a hard time

keepin' You in my focus,

Lord, You need to let me know

when I need to tune in to You.

Sometimes I don't even notice

it when I drift away.

I know what I'm gonna say for a second,

and then I get distracted by my thoughts.

I don't know why it happens to me that quickly.

Why do I easily forget?

It bums me up,

'cause this is somethin' I've been goin' through

for a very long time,

and I need You to heal this head of mine.

So let me get down and dirty

Antonio Finn

on my knees right now.

While in my situation,

I need to do some serious prayin'.

Yeah, right.

It'll be more like cryin' out loud,

Lord, I believe You'll do it for me.

I don't need to see a sign.

You, Lord, are who I want

constantly on my mind.

At times, it seems like my mind

is racing a hundred miles an hour.

How can I expect to get rid

of all of these problems?

Pretty soon they'll devour me if

I'm not careful.

If I had my mind on You, Lord,

who's my strong tower.

I'd appreciate it if You'd drench me

in Your awesome healing power.

Sometimes you just have to stop thinkin'

Spiritual Lyrics

about your problems

and just stop to smell the roses

or any kind of flower.

I'm tired of my mind being locked up in bondage,

when He died on the cross for this reason.

So my mind can be in perfect peace.

If only my mind can be stayed on Thee.

Antonio Finn

1-7-05 SCATTERED FLOCK

Spiritual Lyrics

The shepherd watches over his sheep

twenty-four/seven all around the clock,

'cause the enemy

that's dressed up in sheep's clothing

is watchin' us like a hawk.

His interest is to upset the shepherd,

and it's him he wants to mock.

Why I don't know.

It doesn't take a lot of effort.

If he can just get one sheep to turn away

then he would've done his job,

then there would be a scattered flock.

It's okay,

'cause he'll leave the ninety-nine

to get the one that has gone astray.

It doesn't even matter where he may be,

the shepherd will make sure

it doesn't happen again.

This time the sheep will stay.

What he has to do for his sheep

Antonio Finn

to make him obey

might seem kinda harsh,

but it's not.

I don't think that I could do it.

It takes so much courage on the shepherd's part.

A little tap will do it.

It's just like crackin' an egg open.

I rather have it done that way

instead of fallin' off a ledge.

It won't even stop the shepherd

from breakin' the sheep's legs

no matter how the sheep cries

or how much he'll beg.

The sheep will be around his master's neck

without a choice,

and it may wonder

what is that mufflin' sound

or what's that noise.

It'll be the sound that from now on

the sheep will recognize.

Spiritual Lyrics

It's the shepherd's voice.

I'll say it again.

The shepherd watches his sheep

twenty-four/ seven around the clock,

'cause the enemy,

that's dressed up in sheep's clothing,

is watchin' us like a hawk.

His only interest is to upset the shepherd,

and it's him he wants to mock.

Why I don't know.

It doesn't take a lot

if he can just get one sheep to turn away,

then he would have done his job,

and then there would be a scattered flock.

If you'd just follow his voice,

it won't happen.

I think not.

Antonio Finn

11-15-04   WERE YOU THERE?

Spiritual Lyrics

I have to get this off my mind,

so why don't ya pull up a chair?

This is directed to the people

who never were real

were there for me and who

continually tried to dictate my life.

I've got just a few words for you

that I'd like to share.

Let's go back to the day I was first born.

Everything seemed fine then,

other than the fact that my mom

was a little bit tired and torn.

Some words came to her

from the doctor that were startlin',

like a very loud horn, sayin' to her,

"We don't know if he'll be able to go home,

because somethin' is definitely wrong with him."

If my mom had her way,

she would've said, "I'm outta here. So long."

In reality she was feelin' so sick,

Antonio Finn

plus the meds she was on messed her all up.

The question is,

"Were you there?"

I'm not gonna hold any of my words

back from ya.

You I will not spare,

and you control my life.

You couldn't even try to

give me any encouraging words.

Yeah, ya didn't with me share,

and you didn't even check on me

to see how I was doin'.

If you didn't know,

I had many burdens to bear.

But, thanks to God I'm still here.

He never runs out of His mercy and grace

He continually gives.

God's not dead.

He still lives,

and His word is very much alive.

Spiritual Lyrics

It's still active.

I know God was there for me,

but I don't recall seein' you anywhere.

Right now it's just a blank stare.

Do you remember those times

that you knew all of the trials

I was goin' through?

Did you even think about me?

Why didn't you say a pull about me?

Did you even care?

All of the times you probably was glad

I got caught up in a bind, ya know a snare,

but let me tell ya God always has been there,

especially all of the times I felt scared.

He released me every time

out of the enemy's traps.

I was snared.

Lord, many times I've been spared!

Ask this question that's directed

toward whomever it may concern.

Antonio Finn

Were You there?

Spiritual Lyrics

12-9-04 TRUST THE WORD

Antonio Finn

Can ya believe what it says?

You know that great Book

that has all of the nouns and verbs.

It's tellin' us that we were created for God

to worship or serve Him,

so let's get ourselves together.

Go ahead and up we gird.

Do you trust what the Bible says?

Do ya trust the Lord's word?

I don't know about you,

but I'm gonna trust in it.

It's steerin' me straight ahead.

There's no need for you to tickle my ears

when you talk to me,

'cause everything you've said better be right,

and I better be able to relate to it.

I'm gonna see for myself

and not just take your word for it.

Oh yes, I know I've got to investigate.

After the Word clears everything up for me,

Spiritual Lyrics

and you're proven wrong,

then we can't even converse anymore.

What can be more honest than the gospel?

Even though the disciples had some doubt,

they still managed to start trustin' in it.

Man, I tell ya those apostles were something else.

They used the Word to get

out of their many binds and obstacles.

You can do it, too.

The Word can help you from bills, marriage, and finances.

It can even help you get up out of that bed

that's at the hospital. Saints,

can you picture this?

God is the ship,

and we're the seamen that trust in the Word

which is our nautical guide.

It works on land, too.

If you don't really trust in what I'm sayin',

just look for the story in the Bible

about the son who was a prodigal.

Antonio Finn

I dare you to just try the Word out,

and get yourself a King James version,

'cause some Bibles aren't what they're perceived to be

with a lot of missing chapters and verses no wonder.

That's why you still grieve.

One of you got one that's watered down.

Just leave it right there behind,

and start what you've been wanting

for all these years.

Now you can achieve it.

The true word is what you should

be having in your hand

for you to receive God's blessings.

As long as you believe in yourself,

you can do it.

You wicked doers can't tell me a lie,

'cause I follow what's true.

It's been around forever and is really old.

It's not new.

I'm gonna make sure I cleave to it

Spiritual Lyrics

all of my days like glue.

In the Word I'll forever trust,

'cause it won't steer me wrong

as I already discussed earlier.

It's either do what's right or burn to dust.

As for me, I choose to do right.

It's a must.

Antonio Finn

11-20-04 TRUE LOVE

Spiritual Lyrics

I can't help it, Lord,

but I have to talk about You.

You know how Your love is so real

and how You managed to bring me through.

When I was in the world, Father,

Your angels watched over me

'cause You knew I needed a helping hand.

I couldn't have gotten any love like this

from any other man.

They're too busy marrying

or worrying about material things,

like how to get a little piece of land.

They'll even tell you to your face

how they stand,

and if they did something for me.

I'm sure I'll have to hear it again.

You see, Lord, that's why

I'm glad I have You.

Father, Your love is so real,

it stays true and fresh each and every day

Antonio Finn

as the early morning dew.

Lord, there're some people in my life

who love me, too.

I can count on two hands.

There're only a handful or a few.

Their love can't touch You.

What kind of man is this?

He made a plan for me,

and He thought about me when I didn't even exist.

Who was betrayed for me with a little kiss.

He also took stripes for my sake.

He died on the cross

with nails stickin' through His wrists.

I remember the time You waited for me,

and the gentleman that You are, Lord,

You waited patiently.

I can hear You tellin' the devil

he'll come around You.

Just wait and see.

Now that's true love.

Spiritual Lyrics

It has got to be.

Lord, Your love is so true,

and it's not fake.

It's the same as it was yesterday.

Even when I open my eyes and wake,

Your true love is there for me.

Even when I make a mess of things

and make many mistakes.

The Lord's love is true,

'cause I don't know anyone else

who still will come through for me

when I still mess up things.

How about you?

Some people may come close,

maybe a handful or a selective few.

Oh no, let me back it up, Lord.

Nobody even comes close to Your true love.

Antonio Finn

12-26-04 BABY JESUS

Spiritual Lyrics

Who knew that our help would come

through a woman who was a virgin.

One day she was visited by God's messenger

who was chosen by God for certain.

To her these words were very discouraging,

so she replied, "How can this be when

I don't even know a man?"

Nevertheless, the messenger told her

she wouldn't do this alone.

She'll have a host

by her side and,

He'd be there when she needed him most.

He's a wonderful comfort,

and He's called the Holy Ghost.

After registering himself and his wife,

Joseph returned to Bethlehem.

Mary was with child.

Her husband knew she was about to deliver.

The situation looked slim.

There was no place for them to go,

Antonio Finn

and no room at the inn.

How would you feel if it was your wife?

Could you imagine the anger he felt?

Finally, someone took pity on

Joseph and his wife, Mary.

The Lord sent a stranger to rescue them,

so Mary could deliver Baby Jesus

in a small area where cattle and horses fed.

It was a manger.

Baby Jesus was wrapped up in swaddling clothes.

Please don't ask me why,

'cause I don't know.

If you ask me not questions,

I'll tell you no lies.

I thank you, God, for bringing a Savior

that for all our sins He did die.

Who knew that our help would come

Through a woman who was a virgin,

who was blessed among all women

and who was blessed by God.

Spiritual Lyrics

That's for certain.

But to her these words were discouragin'.

"How could this be when I know not a man?"

she replied.

Little did Mary know

God had it already worked out.

He had a good plan.

Lord God, You don't need us,

but we all need You.

We're so sorry that it takes so much work

to please us.

I can't speak for anyone else,

But, Lord, thanks for Baby Jesus.

Antonio Finn

11-24-04   THINKIN' POSITIVE

Spiritual Lyrics

You're probably wondering why things

aren't working out right for you.

Some things have to change.

Somewhere right upstairs are those

bad thoughts in your brain.

Somehow your thoughts have to be rearranged.

Instead of thinkin' negative

you need to believe in yourself

that everything will be okay.

Take it by force and be very aggressive.

It's really all up to you.

Don't you know that God has all power?

There's no limit to it,

'cause His power is excessive.

Now isn't that pretty impressive?

There's nothin' wrong with positive thinkin'

if you could just get it through your head,

maybe you'd stop sinkin'.

You can try covering things up,

but that won't do you any good.

Antonio Finn

Stop the smokin' and the drinkin'.

Today, start thinkin' positive.

Some things may not go your way,

and people who are around you

might mistreat you,

or they may talk negative about you.

With such talk you need to quickly reject it

and be very objective toward them

right then and there.

Your memory needs to be selective,

'cause if you don't act positive pretty soon,

those folks will get you to start actin'

just like them, very negative.

What I need from you, brothers and sisters,

right now is for you to be very receptive.

Please take heed to my words,

and reject the negative thinkin',

so you can think positive.

Of your good thoughts

you should be very protective.

Spiritual Lyrics

Like me, I know you're tired of things

not goin' your way,

and you're tired of losin' to the enemy.

Today why don't you be possessive

and go out and take by force

everything the enemy stole from you?

Get it back for once in your life.

Be aggressive and think the opposite of negative.

You should be think positive.

Antonio Finn

1-5-05 THINGS ARE GETTING BETTER

Spiritual Lyrics

After all I've been through,

finally things are gettin' better.

I remember at one time

I was weighed down

with all of my burdens.

They were so much heavier

than they are now.

Thanks to You, God,

my burdens are light as a feather.

All of the credit goes to You,

'cause, Lord, you were the only one

who helped me put it all together.

I remember at one point in time,

I didn't even think I stood a chance

up against all of my problems.

Despite that, I had to continue on through,

no matter the circumstance.

At the sight of trouble every once in a while,

You may see me take a quick look or glance

and see me praise God, anyway.

Antonio Finn

I feel the urge to kick up my heels

like King David did.

I want to dance.

Some people might not agree

with the things which I share.

I can hear them now sayin'

how dare he talk about all of the times

that he was in so much despair?

Do you really want to know

why I compare certain situations

to what's goin' on now?

It's to remind myself that the Lord is still able

and that He still cares.

He was the only one who was around.

This is directed toward all those who criticized me.

Anyway, you weren't even there.

Lord, I appreciate everything

that You've done for me

and for all of the food, clothing, and shelter.

At one point of time in my life,

Spiritual Lyrics

my burdens weighed me down.

They were so much heavier,

but now, Lord, thanks to You,

they're lighter than a feather.

All the credit is due unto You

for puttin' things together for me.

If things aren't goin' as you've planned,

just keep this in mind.

Pretty soon things are gonna get better.

www.ingramcontent.com/pod-product-compliance
Lightning Source LLC
Chambersburg PA
CBHW080410170426
43194CB00015B/2764